Young Jerry Ford

Young Jerry Ford

ATHLETE AND CITIZEN

Hendrik Booraem V

William B. Eerdmans Publishing Company

Grand Rapids, Michigan / Cambridge, U.K.

Published 2013 by
Wm. B. Eerdmans Publishing Co.
2140 Oak Industrial Drive N.E., Grand Rapids, Michigan 49505 /
P.O. Box 163, Cambridge CB3 9PU U.K.

Printed in the United States of America

18 17 16 15 14 13   7 6 5 4 3 2 1

ISBN 978-0-8028-6942-5

www.eerdmans.com

Contents

Foreword, by Hank Meijer   vii

Preface: A Superior Type of Young Man   ix

Acknowledgments   xiii

1. How Leslie L. King Jr. Came to Grand Rapids   3

2. Climbing the Ladder of Success   21

3. Willingly to School   41

4. Playing by the Rules   57

5. Friends and Fun   75

6. "Hey, Whitey, You're a Center"   87

7. The Athlete   99

8. Leadership, Law, and the Depression   115

Conclusion   127

Index   133

Foreword

Jerry Ford was not born Jerry Ford. Thereon hangs a tale unlike any other in the annals of presidential biography. The exotic and dramatic story of his origins yields to the more familiar story of his all-American youth in a happy corner of the Midwest. It also colors that familiar story in ways that enrich our understanding of this most underrated leader of the free world. The narrative is one of family, in all its complex permutations, and it bears all the reassuring hallmarks of faith and fortitude and good feeling that we hunger for in our leaders.

President Ford restored the good name of the United States in a time of crisis. He was not a man whose temperament was given to brooding or doubt, anxiety or sleeplessness. But in his later years, in Colorado or California, when he couldn't sleep, he told his friend, presidential biographer Richard Norton Smith, he would lie awake at night "and think of Grand Rapids" as if evoking a comfortable dream.

He was not born in Grand Rapids, just as he was not born Jerry Ford. But Grand Rapids became his hometown when he was very young. Its iconic Midwestern sobriety and earnestness went a long way toward defining him. It nurtured and sheltered him. It eventually sent him to Congress as its representative—over and over. He repaid his constituents with hard work, from personal responses to their letters and requests to inspiring appearances at every occasion, from the Red Flannel Days parade to the smallest school assembly. He served the town and the town, in turn, gave him a place to which he could always go home again.

Hendrik Booraem's story of the young Gerald Ford is a powerful testament to the way nature and nurture — and in some ways nature giving way to nurture — come together to form who we are. Tracing the childhood of our thirty-eighth president is a detective story as well as a retelling of familiar truths. Booraem, who has previously published youth biographies of Presidents Andrew Jackson, William Henry Harrison, James Garfield, and Calvin Coolidge, does a masterful job of discerning in Ford's youth the seeds of character that would alter American history.

His mother and stepfather provided the secure support that fostered a confident young man. Their home had three rules: work hard, tell the truth, and show up for dinner on time. The Boy Scouts, South High School, and an uneven gridiron, where a young athlete proved his toughness and prowess, provided settings where a powerful personality could begin to assert itself. As Speaker of the United States House of Representatives Thomas P. ("Tip") O'Neill observed of his good friend across the aisle, the country was fortunate to have President Ford in its grave moment of constitutional peril in the 1970s just as it was fortunate to have Abraham Lincoln during the agony of the Civil War in the 1860s.

Reflecting on West Michigan's native son in this the centennial year of his birth (2013), it is altogether appropriate that we revisit his roots as we celebrate his legacy. Where did Gerald Ford *come from*? What resources did he draw upon when he found himself so suddenly crossing the threshold of the White House as its unelected occupant? We are lucky indeed to have Hendrik Booraem's account of how where he came from shaped who he became.

HANK MEIJER

Preface: A Superior Type of Young Man

The FBI recruiter who, in Grand Rapids, Michigan, in July 1941, interviewed twenty-eight-year-old Gerald R. Ford about a job, was impressed with the man opposite him. He "appeared to be a superior type of young man," he wrote on the report. "It is obvious that his home life and breeding were exceptional." In his statement, the agent, Wilson McFarlin, chose not to highlight some of the applicant's most spectacular qualifications — his husky build, his blond good looks, his Yale law degree, his outstanding athletic record as a player and assistant coach, or his status as a promising young lawyer in the city. He focused instead on home life and values. Ford was a "superior *type* of young man" — that is, he had been brought up right, by committed parents who knew what they were about. In July 1941 there were probably scores of such fine young men all over the Midwest, fortunate enough to have had strong, loving parents and stable backgrounds. But only one of them would go on to become president of the United States.

The connection between the presidency, on the one hand, and high principles and good character, on the other, has always been a bit loose. People get to the White House for many good reasons, of which character is only one, and generally not the most important. Presidents are doers, speakers, performers, exponents of a point of view, often promoters of an agenda. Such traits as truthfulness, integrity, self-restraint, and commitment to principle in connection with these goals are to some degree optional, and their connection to chief executives of the United States has been intermittent. Occupants of the office who displayed too many of them have sometimes been labeled "Boy Scouts," executives too virtuous in character to be effective leaders. (Ford, not coincidentally, was a devoted Boy Scout.) Many people can have good character, but when one is looking for individual excellence, it is not necessarily a recommendation to have something that many people share. There is special satisfaction in studying a president whose life blended the individual drive that propels one to high office with the social responsibility of being a good, exemplary person in the eyes of one's peers — a nice guy who succeeded.

That is what this book does as it follows the early life of Gerald Ford, who was certainly not the only U.S. president to have been both a leader and a good citizen, but who offers a near-perfect example of the type. He was also an admirable, likable human being, a man whose childhood offers glimpses of family and school, sports, recreation, and western Michigan life in the Jazz Age and the Depression. A study of Ford's early years provides insights into how the values of good character are created and reinforced by networks of family, friends, and community institutions.

Athletics, too, played a part in shaping Jerry Ford's values. The time of his boyhood coincided with the rise of sports in America to an important model of behavior for middle-class American males. To follow his schoolboy career is to sense the power of community involvement and community approval, and to see American sport in a distant mirror — innocent and idealistic compared to its later developments. It is to relive a fresh, energetic era that was working out the concept of playing by the rules to achieve large-scale success. The athletic picture of the 1920s and 1930s is so varied and full of new developments that a reader can lose track of the main point: that Jerry Ford was developing — on the playing fields and courts of the period — the drives, principles, and habits of mind he would bring to the White House in a troubled era.

Finally, at the edges of this story, in its later years, lurks the Great Depression, the ultimate character-testing experience, which left its stamp on almost all Americans who experienced it. Jerry Ford graduated from high school in the first really serious year of the Depression, and this book explores how he responded to its challenges, even as it sketches the impact of economic crisis on an earlier America in some ways very different from ours.

GERALD FORD AND HIS FAMILY made this book possible by generously depositing a large collection of documents in the Gerald R. Ford Presidential Library: photos both formal and informal, papers that range from family scrapbooks to government documents, and reporters' interviews of Ford's old friends and acquaintances. Together with his own memoir, *A Time to Heal,* and the interviews he gave to his official biographer, James Cannon, these papers create a vivid picture of the future president from early childhood to high-school graduation. They are the single most important source for this narrative. The staff of the presidential library in Ann Arbor, where most of the printed materials and photos are kept, has been generous with time and expertise in helping identify all the sources, written and pictorial. The presidential museum in Grand Rapids also has important items.

In addition, Richard Ford, President Ford's surviving brother, who has given numerous interviews over the years, shared some of his memories one more time with me for this book.

Next in importance are the collections of the Grand Rapids Public Library, Local History Department. They exist to provide a portrait of the city as it grew and developed over the years, often with reminiscences, interviews, and specialized sketches of different people and institutions. These are essential background for understanding Jerry Ford and his family. City newspapers from the period, especially the *Grand Rapids Herald,* have items about the family, the neighborhood, the high school, and sometimes Ford himself. I owe the Grand Rapids Public Library staff a great debt for helping me use this large collection, especially the photographs.

Back in 1997-1998, two dozen men and women from Ford's high school class shared with me their memories of him and of South High School, adding flashes of recollection from their experience that have enhanced my story of his high school years. I want particularly to acknowledge the contributions of Arnold Sisson, Florence Moore Johnson, Marshall Reister, Kenneth Hayes, Sid Nadolsky, Melvin Barclay, Bill Schuiling, Tena Sikkema Streeter, and Dorothy Gray Guck of the Class of 1931, and Harold Bosscher of the Class of 1932.

Several Grand Rapidians contributed their knowledge in specialized areas to make this book better, and they deserve special thanks: Tim J. Todish, on Boy Scouting in western Michigan; Chris Carron, on the furniture industry; Rick Williams, on Masonic lodges and traditions; Dan Aument, on the history of Ottawa Beach; and Tim England, on the Fords' Union Avenue home.

The Gerald R. Ford Foundation has underwritten the illustrations that are the core of this book. Their promise of support at an earlier stage was instrumental in getting this project started for the centennial celebration. Others who have contributed to the book in important ways have been Mike Grass, who played a vital role in getting it started; Hendrik Meijer; Bob France of Nunica, Michigan; Donald Holloway of the Ford Museum; and Professor Matthew Rusnak of Rutgers University and Bucks County Community College. Brian Nugent produced the map of Ford's childhood world.

As always, my most important debt as an author is to my life partner, Richard Bullock.

Acknowledgments

The author and publisher gratefully acknowledge permission to reproduce illustrations from the following sources:

Images on pages 2, 4, 5, 6, 7, 8, 11, 30, 31, 37, 38, 40, 44-45, 46, 47, 56, 66, 67, 70, 71, 72, 73, 74, 76, 79, 84, 86, 91, 98, 100, 103, 105, 108, 109, 114, 119: courtesy of the Gerald R. Ford Library.

Images on pages 10, 15, 17, 22, 24, 26, 27, 29, 35, 42, 43, 48, 51, 80, 85, 100, 120, 122: courtesy of Grand Rapids History & Special Collections, Archives, Grand Rapids Public Library, Grand Rapids, Michigan.

The image of Michigan Stadium in the 1920s on page 102: courtesy of Wilfrid Byron Shaw Papers, Bentley Historical Library, University of Michigan.

The map on page 20: courtesy of Brian Nugent.

The photograph on page 9: courtesy of Anderson Collection, Caspar College Western History Center.

The photograph on page 69, taken by Virgil D. Haynes: courtesy of Emil Lorch Papers, Bentley Historical Library, University of Michigan.

Reproductions of pages from the Scout Handbook of 1927 on pages 62-65: courtesy of the Boy Scouts of America.

Young Jerry Ford

A young
Leslie L. King Jr.
portrayed as
being in Florida

1 How Leslie L. King Jr. Came to Grand Rapids

Chance plays a part in every human life, but it took an amazing string of coincidences to send little Leslie King Jr. to Grand Rapids, Michigan, to change his name to Gerald R. Ford Jr., and eventually to become thirty-eighth president of the United States. In coming to Grand Rapids to live, he acquired more than a new name, a new father, and a new home. Arguably, he acquired a new personality and a new set of values — in short, a new self. This first part of his story is worth retelling because it suggests the contrast, more extreme in Ford's life than in most, between what was and what might have been.

IN HARVARD, ILLINOIS, in September 1912, in the village Episcopal church, the former mayor's daughter, twenty-year-old Dorothy Ayer Gardner, married the tall, blond, charming brother of a college friend. The dark-haired bride was beautiful; her groom, twenty-eight-year-old Leslie Lynch King of Omaha, was the son of a wealthy western merchant, and he worked in his father's wool business. Both the bride's parents — ambitious and hard-headed businessman Levi Gardner and proud, ancestry-conscious Adele Gardner — had given the match their blessing. It seemed to be an idyllic wedding.

Dorothy Gardner King as a new bride, September 1912

Within days of the ceremony, however, the dream disintegrated. King struck his beautiful bride twice on their honeymoon and repeatedly threatened more violence. Beneath his big-talking façade, it turned out, he was an angry and unstable young man. Moreover, though he worked for his father, the two were not close: Charles King gave his son no support, and the latter was in debt. Appalled by the violence and the other things she was learning about Leslie, Dorothy left her husband in Omaha and went back to Illinois. He followed her to ask for a second chance. She agreed. By late fall the couple was living unhappily in a basement apartment in Omaha, Leslie was drinking immoderately, and the routine of threats and blows had started again. In December, Dorothy discovered that she was pregnant.

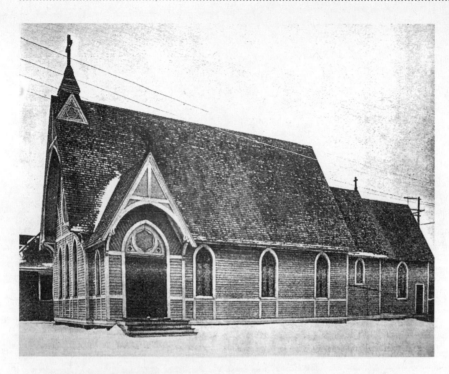

Christ Church, Harvard, Illinois, where Dorothy Gardner and Leslie L. King were married

Trying to make the marriage work for the baby's sake, and embarrassed at the thought of returning home in her condition, Dorothy King endured months of her husband's ill temper and violent outbursts. Charles King, despite his arms-length relationship with his son, agreed to allow his grand Victorian house on Woolworth Avenue to be used for the delivery of the baby; he also provided for a nurse and a doctor, while he and his wife left town.

Adele Gardner came from Harvard to be with her daughter. Doubtless they both hoped that the birth could transform the marriage. On July 14, the hottest day of the summer of 1913, the baby arrived safely and in good health, a little boy whom they named Leslie Junior.

The day after the little boy's birth, the nightmare began again. King took offense at his mother-in-law's presence, and he ordered the doctor and nurse to leave. According to Mrs. Gardner, King then threatened to shoot his wife and child. Apparently reluctant to call

Leslie Lynch King

the police because of the King family's social position, the women telegraphed Levi Gardner, who made the twelve-hour train trip from Chicago. King was more reasonable with Dorothy's father: the marriage was a failure, he said, and he agreed to a separation as soon as Dorothy and the baby were rested enough to leave. With his mission accomplished, Gardner returned to his real-estate business in Chicago.

With Leslie King, however, nothing was simple. A few days after

Charles King's house in Omaha, where Leslie L. King Jr. was born

his father-in-law left, he began brandishing a butcher knife. The nurse called the police. But King then secured a court order forbidding his wife access to either of her parents, making her a virtual prisoner. She escaped by slipping out of the house with the baby and taking a hired carriage across the river to Council Bluffs, Iowa, where her parents were awaiting her. On the last day of July, less than a year after her wedding, Dorothy returned home to Harvard, Illinois, with her two-week-old baby. In December she was granted a divorce. King was ordered to pay the then substantial amount of twenty-five dollars a month in child support, plus three thousand dollars alimony; but, pleading poverty, he paid nothing. From Dorothy's point of view, at least the traumatic marriage was over, and she could get on with her life.

Chicago seemed like a logical place for a new start. Her father had an office there, and her married sister, Tannisse James, lived in the suburbs. After a brief stay with her sister and brother-in-law,

7

Adele Gardner with three grandsons; Gerald Ford Jr. at right

Dorothy found a job as a saleswoman and a place to live in Hyde Park, near the old Columbian Exposition fairgrounds. She moved in there with her little son, whom she had taken to calling Junior. Dorothy's parents also left Harvard; but rather than staying in the Chicago area, they moved into a large, comfortable house on the far south side of Grand Rapids, Michigan, where Mr. Gardner's firm had long had an office. That arrangement, however, lasted for only a short time. Soon after they had moved to Grand Rapids, Levi Gardner was diagnosed with Bright's disease (kidney failure).

Adele Gardner needed help caring for her husband and accompanying him to the various spas and clinics where they went for treatment. Dorothy and Junior were frequently summoned to Grand Rapids, and they also accompanied Adele and Levi on trips to Florida and Missouri. There are photos of Junior in a white sailor suit on a walk lined with palm trees. By the time Levi Gardner died,

in May of 1916 — less than two years after his grandson's birth — Dorothy had given up her Chicago job to become her mother's full-time assistant. By that time, Charles King had begun sending her the court-ordered child support of twenty-five dollars a month that his son had never paid. So Dorothy stayed in Grand Rapids with Junior, listing herself in the city directory as a young widow.

Charles H. King (far left), Leslie's father; Leslie is third from left.

Mother and daughter began putting down roots in the way two educated, respectable women would do — through clubs and churches. They joined the Daughters of the American Revolution on the strength of Adele's Ayer ancestry, and boasted of a list of contributions their forebears had made to the history of New England and the Midwest.

They began attending a charming little Episcopal church, Grace Church, on the near South Side. There, within a few months, Dorothy caught the eye of a serious young man who lived near the church, where he and his mother and sister were communicants. His name was Gerald R. (Jerry) Ford, and like many Grand Rapids men, he

Grace Episcopal Church, Grand Rapids, in its old location on Lafayette Avenue

worked in a business related to furniture and design, selling paint and wallpaper for Heystek and Canfield, a well-known downtown firm. Gerald and Dorothy met at a church social, and they began seeing each other regularly.

Ford's family was from a slightly lower social level than were the Gardners. There were no rich people in it, not even in memory. Ford's father had been killed in a tragic accident when Gerald and his three sisters were very young, and he had dropped out of school after the eighth grade in order to support his widowed mother and his sisters. But that background did not matter to Dorothy. Jerry was personally attractive: tall, friendly, steady, and even tempered. The latter two qualities counted for a good deal with Dorothy, whose first marriage was to the spoiled son of a wealthy family. Experience had taught her to value steadiness over wealth. There are indications, however, that social class did matter to her mother. Whatever the reason, Dorothy did not rush into marriage. She and Gerald Ford did not get married until February 1917, and then the wedding was not held in Grace Church but near the groom's home on Madison Avenue. Dorothy, her mother, and Leslie King (whom the family simply called "Junior") went to live at Jerry Ford's rented home, 716 Madison Avenue, in a somewhat less classy neighborhood than they were used to. Jerry's mother and a sister lived in the other half of the two-family house.

For Dorothy, it was the beginning of a long and very happy marriage. Her son remained "Junior"; but from then on he was no longer Junior King, but Junior Ford. Years later, in high school, he decided he wanted to be called "Jerry" like his father — in other words, Gerald R. Ford Jr. — though that did not become his *legal* name until he graduated from the University of Michigan. As he began his adult life with a coaching position at Yale University, Jerry decided that the time had come to make it official, to recognize the man who had

Gerald R. Ford Sr.

11

made him who he was. On December 3, 1935, Leslie L. King Jr. finally — legally and officially — became Gerald R. Ford Jr.

Buffeted by the storms of family misfortune and the moves from
Omaha to Oak Park to Chicago to Grand Rapids, Dorothy guarded
her handsome blond-haired child, hoping like any young mother
that her love could envelop him in a protective shield. Finally, in
1917, settled with Jerry Ford, she could take stock of Junior and see
how the years of upheaval had affected him. Physically, she saw no
problems: he was healthy and strong. But temperament was a different story. In Junior she saw the sudden irrational flashes of temper
that had wrecked her first marriage. Like Leslie King, he would get
red-faced and strike out or throw things if he didn't get his way. In
1918 she enrolled him in the public kindergarten, where the teacher
recalled him years later as "naughty Junior Ford" — a little trouble-
maker who slammed the door when he went out and once pushed
another boy through it.

Junior had to be taught to control his temper. Since neither Dorothy nor Jerry believed in physical punishment, they used reason
and psychology. When the boy exploded at home, his mother would
put him in front of a mirror and point out how silly he looked, or she
would laugh at his fits of anger and try to tease him out of them. His
stepfather's approach was more serious and straightforward, the
classic motivational talk. Since both parents were dedicated Chris-
tians, they turned to the Bible for help. They gave Junior a Bible
verse to memorize, Proverbs 16:32: "He that is slow to anger is better
than the mighty, and he that ruleth his spirit than he that taketh a
city." Later, he learned Rudyard Kipling's poem "If" by heart. The
first two lines of that poem are: "If you can keep your head when all
about you / Are losing theirs, and blaming it on you . . ."

The hard-fought struggle for anger management lasted through
the boy's whole early life, through college and beyond, and — with
the help of sports, which I will examine later — was ultimately a
near-total success. By the time Ford was in high school he was close
enough to mastery for the whole story of his epic temper to become

part of family folklore, with various stories on the subject, for instance, wrapping his golf club around a tree and similar incidents. "My very young years, I had a terrible temper," he told a biographer in the White House, when his violent reactions were comfortably in the past, thanks to the love and systematic attention he received from his parents.

While that battle was underway, another developed. Junior was in the second grade when he began to have problems with stuttering. He could begin to form words but not get them out. Various versions exist of how long the problem lasted — he changed elementary schools twice in those years — but its effects were understandable: unsure whether he would be able to utter a word successfully, he spoke less and less. He acquired the image he would have throughout his school years: a very quiet youngster, friendly but not verbal. Some teachers called him shy. At last one grade-school teacher realized that the speaking difficulty was really a problem related to learning to write: Junior was naturally a left-hander, but the school system, as was customary at the time, was forcing him to write right-handed. As soon as he was allowed to use his left hand for writing, the stuttering went away. His taciturn nature, however, remained.

Ford wrote left-handed for the rest of his life, using the position teachers call "the hook," with the left forearm awkwardly curled over the top of the writing surface. His writing was distinctive, but not hard to read. He was a lefty at meals, too. His right-handed family soon got used to giving him one whole side of the dinner table to avoid collisions. But in sports he pitched, passed, or dribbled the ball with his right hand. As he liked to tell interviewers, he was left-handed sitting down and right-handed standing up.

The outbursts of rage, the difficulties with speaking and writing, combine to suggest that perhaps Ford did carry some psychological baggage from the tempestuous environment of his early years. By the time he reached his teens, however, it was largely under control, thanks to the love and care of his parents, particularly of his mother.

13

Dorothy Gardner Ford was an extraordinary woman. "I get my energy from my mother," Ford said as president.

"She was a tremendously energetic person, just fantastic. She probably had more friends than any woman I ever knew. Everybody loved her. She was a human dynamo in a womanly way. She wasn't a great career type. But she was the most thoughtful person, always writing to people — a note on a birthday — or calling on some who were in the hospital." Dorothy loved to entertain, give gifts, and organize bridge clubs. She related easily to others, and wept easily.

As the wife of Jerry Ford, she had three more sons: Tom, born in 1918; Dick, in 1924; and Jim, in 1927. She regretted the lack of a daughter, because of her love for dolls and decorations, but at Christmas time and in her Episcopal church guild, she had some chance to express those interests. At home, with hungry males to feed, she took on the traditional domestic roles with zest. In the kitchen, she baked molasses cookies, Christmas treats, and blueberry tarts. Her sons' friends loved the sweet, appetizing smell of the Ford kitchen when they stepped inside. Fond of her own cooking, Dorothy put on weight during the course of the 1920s, and she eventually developed health problems.

Dorothy Ford had high moral standards for her sons. She loved them dearly and had definite expectations for their behavior. They were to pray every night, attend church regularly, and read their Bible — not to lie, or smoke, or drink. For good works, they had her constant example of gifts, calls, committee work, and notes. She followed their interests. When Junior became involved in high-school football, for example, she began filling a scrapbook with clippings and photos. She was a steady, dependable presence in their lives.

All the qualities that Jerry and Dorothy sought to instill in their sons were influenced by one major factor: the Ford household was a religious one, and religious in a way that suited Junior's temperament. There was grace before meals, daily Bible reading, family devotions led by his father, and prayer at night. There was no meditation, no discussion, no posturing — just simple, nondogmatic action. The feeling and the conviction were there, as they were in the orderly Episcopal worship services the Fords attended, with their hymns and responses. Dorothy's dolls and candy and get-well notes, as well as Jerry's civic clubs and his study of political issues — all these seemed to be outgrowths of these beliefs, conviction translated into purposeful activity. "I am most reluctant to speak or write about [my religion]," a mature Gerald Ford Jr. would later say. "They didn't talk religion," a family friend said, "they just lived it."

JUNIOR WAS SIXTEEN YEARS OLD when he unexpectedly met his biological father. He had begun calling himself "Jerry" by that time, although to his mother he was still "Junior" and always would be. An eleventh-grader at South High School in Grand Rapids, he worked at lunchtime and one night a week in a snack shop called Bill's Place, across Hall Street from the school, for the sum of $2.00 a week, plus lunch.

Bill's Place in 1930, the hamburger shack where Ford worked during high school

It was the spring of 1930, April or May. Jerry's paternal biological

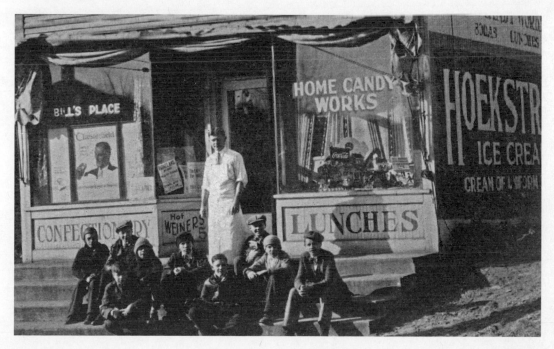

15

grandfather, Charles King, whom he had never met, had died earlier that spring, and the child support checks had stopped. Perhaps his mother had told him nothing about that. The money was no longer critical.

At lunchtime Bill's was usually crowded with students, hungry not only for its hamburgers but also for the specialty of the house, fresh-baked sticky cinnamon rolls. Jerry, in his apron, was busy at the grill or collecting money at the register, dependably quiet and easy-going. But there were lulls, and during one of them Jerry became aware of a customer he had never seen before, a large, sandy-haired man, well dressed, standing near the door as he gave the place an appraising once-over. He did not at all resemble the typical Bill's Place customer.

The man approached the counter and looked Jerry in the eye. "Are you Leslie King?"

"No," Jerry said.

"Are you Jerry Ford?"

"Yes."

"You're Leslie King. I'm your father. You don't know me. I'd like to take you to lunch."

This seemed like total nonsense, but the man was an apparently sane adult. Jerry thought a moment and recollected his mother's telling him a year or two earlier that she had been previously married, perhaps to a man named King, and that he, Jerry, was connected with that marriage. He had accepted the information without comment: it was probably true, but seemed irrelevant, like ancient history. Now it stood before him.

"I'm working," Jerry temporized.

"Ask your boss if you can get off."

Bill Skougis and his wife Marie had an office in the back of the long, narrow building. Jerry excused himself and went to explain the situation to Bill: "Bill, I've got a personal crisis, can you let me go? I've got to have lunch with this person." Bill said okay, and Jerry took off his apron and put on his coat.

Cherie Inn, where Jerry Ford lunched with his biological father

Outside the shop a classy car was parked, a beautiful new Lincoln, with a woman sitting in the front passenger seat whom King introduced as his wife.

He asked Jerry to recommend a place to eat, and Jerry suggested the Cherie Inn, a small new restaurant several blocks away on the affluent East Side, where South High boys sometimes took their dates. As they drove, King explained to Jerry how he had managed to locate him. He knew he had a son who went by the name Ford attending

17

high school somewhere in Grand Rapids — his strategy was to go to every high school in the city and ask if they had a Leslie King or Junior Ford enrolled there. He was prepared to visit them all, but that proved unnecessary; he found his son on the first or second try. He was passing through the city, he explained, en route to Wyoming, having just bought his new car in Detroit. (Jerry probably did not know enough to connect this purchase with his grandfather's death.)

Over lunch, King asked his son about his football prowess. Jerry told him he had had a good year as a sophomore and had been named to the All-City team. This year a knee problem had slowed him down, but it had been taken care of. Next year he would be team captain. King talked a bit about his wealth and his landholdings in the west. The conversation, Jerry remembered, was "superficial." As he listened, he studied the man opposite him, looking for a physical resemblance. There was some, he had to admit. His mind brimmed with questions: What did King want from him? Why approach him now, after so many years of silence? Merely to see his son, the football hero, and show off his own wealth? But as he told an interviewer years later, "Sometimes you bite your tongue to avoid being impolite."

After their lunch at the Cherie Inn, and as they parted in front of Bill's, King grandly gave Jerry twenty-five dollars. Then he and his wife drove off.

Jerry was preoccupied during afternoon classes and after-school track practice. He knew that he had to tell his parents about the incident, but he was uncertain about how to do that and worried about how they would take it. During dinner, usually a relaxing part of the day, he was tense and uncomfortable.

His fears were unjustified. After dinner, when the younger boys were upstairs, he told his parents what had happened and found them more concerned about his well-being than anything Leslie King might be up to. His mother told him the story of the marriage and divorce in detail. His stepfather reassured him that he had done nothing wrong. Both repeated that they loved and trusted him, and asked him to put the episode behind him. His mother reminded him of a Bible verse he had memorized, Proverbs 3:5: "Trust in the Lord with all thine heart, and lean not unto thine own understanding." The meeting had been part of God's plan, and God would bring it to good.

Later, upstairs in bed, Jerry was still uneasy. For the first time in his life, he had to confront the violence and unpleasantness that underlay his earliest years. He tried in vain to think of something in Leslie King that he could like or respect. Doubtless he tried to trust in the Lord, but it was impossible not to worry about the man's intentions and his potential for disrupting his life in the future.

If what worried Jerry was a possible future of divided loyalties and confused family relations, he was worrying unnecessarily. He and King never became close enough for those to develop. Whatever had motivated King's visit in 1930, it was not paternal concern. That became clear a few years later when Jerry, strapped for cash to continue at the University of Michigan, wrote King to ask for help — and was rejected or ignored. Instead, when he was in law school, he and his mother successfully sued King for the child support he had refused to pay and collected four thousand dollars, with the usual hard feelings. When King died in Tucson in 1941, there were no mourners in the Ford family. Except for the sudden flashes of anger that stayed with him all his life, Jerry, who had begun life as a King, lived it as a 99 percent Ford.

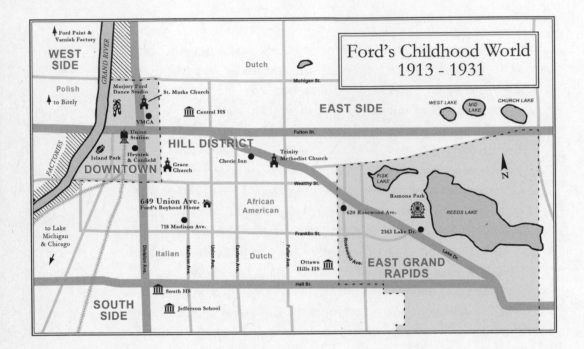

Gerald Ford's childhood world (map by Brian Nugent)

2 Climbing the Ladder of Success

Grand Rapids in the 1920s, when Junior Ford was a boy, was definitely large enough to qualify as a complex modern city. Its population of 137,000 people in 1920 grew to 168,000 in 1930, enough to rank it in both years as forty-seventh or forty-eighth in the country, about the same size as Hartford or Des Moines. Industry rather than commerce or government was its organizing principle: eight major firms and a host of minor ones manufactured furniture and associated products such as lumber, paint, and varnish. Other large companies in the city produced carpet sweepers, church pews, refrigerators, asphalt shingles, and flypaper.

The structure of Grand Rapids was that of any medium-sized American city at that time: a collection of residential neighborhoods, segregated by income and to some extent ethnicity, all linked by public transportation to the central business district — the "downtown" — at the falls of the Grand River. Flowing from north to south, the Grand River divided Grand Rapids into two parts that, by 1920, had grown increasingly dissimilar. Along the river stood the big furniture factories that gave the city its reputation. The men who worked in them mostly lived to the west of the river in dozens of blocks of small homes whose population, during the great waves of immigration just before 1900, gradually changed from An-

glo-American and German to Polish and Lithuanian, ethnic neighborhoods punctuated by Catholic churches and schools. Just east of
the river lay the downtown area, and east of that was a steep hill, the
"Hill District," where the mill owners and the families of prestige
had begun building grand, ornate mansions in the 1880s. Other
members of the "business class," people who worked in the front offices — secretaries, managers, salesmen — tended to live farther to
the east. They were not necessarily rich, but as a rule they valued education and social status. The West Side, broadly speaking, was
working-class, the East Side white-collar.

Public transportation in Grand Rapids meant the brightly
painted electric streetcars of the Grand Rapids Railway Company,
whose network of tracks extended down all the major thoroughfares
in every direction from downtown. Thousands of workers and shoppers rode to and from downtown every day for ten cents a trip. "You
could go anywhere you needed to by taking a streetcar," a doctor's
wife remembered. Passengers could even send letters as they rode,
since each streetcar coach carried a mailbox.

Factories on the Grand River

The rich inhabitants of the city — a 1926 estimate was that it contained thirty-six millionaires — had finer private luxuries in their homes, but the Grand Rapids downtown offered quality fare inexpensively to everyone. The business district was the city's center of commerce and government, but beyond that it stood symbolically for the promise of a city life that could produce high-quality amenities that more than compensated for the discomforts of living in a city that size. The downtown business district meant Herpolsheimer's, the city's leading department store, where a woman played the harp in the quiet, elegant dining room. It meant striking public buildings like the imposing gray-stone City Hall, with its huge bell, and the brand-new Fountain Street Baptist Church. It meant the white-marble Beaux Arts library and the glamorous five-story Pantlind Hotel, with its ballroom and luxury services, the focus of the semiannual Furniture Show. Farther along Lower Monroe were the touring Broadway plays, productions by local companies, vaudeville, burlesque, and the first-run motion picture houses, palatially decorated in the new fashion of the decade, offering a mix of silent films such as "Ben-Hur" and "The Hunchback of Notre Dame." Marjory Ford, Jerry's youngest sister, had her dance studio across from the Pantlind Hotel.

There was the Grand Rapids Symphony, as well as concerts in St. Cecilia Hall. And some of the downtown's greatest pleasures were free: making one's way down the "canyon" of Monroe Street's four- and five-story commercial buildings, with its crowds of secretaries, shoppers, policemen, businessmen, and savoring the illusion of being in a really big city — a Chicago or New York. Or one could stand in the same spot at night looking up at the newly built twelve-story Michigan National Bank Building, where a light flickered way up on the twelfth floor as a cleaning woman passed through, and feeling a sense of big-city grandeur and isolation.

The most important thing to know about Jerry Ford Sr. was this: he had been born on the West Side, but he worked downtown and lived on the East Side. His life goal was to move beyond manual la-

Union Station, Train Shed, Grand Rapids, Mich.

**The train shed
at Union Station**

bor and achieve the status that went with being a man of property. It was certainly no surprise that he saw in Dorothy Gardner King, with her college education and New England ancestry, not just an attractive, lovable woman but a life partner in his quest. Personally, the most important thing was that he was a serious man of high moral ideals. Ford's workplace and his home were the two centers of his existence.

When he and Dorothy began married life, he worked for Heystek and Canfield, on the south end of downtown, near Union Station, where trains from Chicago, Detroit, and the East Coast pulled in under the big semicylindrical train shed. Their home was a two-family house on Madison Avenue just north of Franklin Street, on the southern fringe of the Hill District. Both these locations deserve a closer look.

Heystek and Canfield, like many Grand Rapids businesses, was a specialty business in the general area of home decoration: it sold paint and wallpaper wholesale throughout the Great Lakes and Plains states, and it employed a force of fifteen salesmen. Jerry Ford, thirty years old in 1920, had put in his time on the road; now, as manager of the paint department, he was based at the home office on Commerce Street, strategically close to the terminal. This part of downtown, near Union Station, was a mix of businesses, second-rate hotels, and some fairly disreputable establishments. The real heart of downtown, with its banks and department stores, lay a few blocks north along Monroe Avenue.

Monroe was the transportation hub of the city, where the lines of the Grand Rapids Railway Company converged. As the electrically powered streetcars clanged along Monroe, the street became increasingly crowded during the decade of the 1920s with boxy, black Model T's and other automobiles. Around 1920, when autos began to be popular with city families for use year-round — not just in the summer as toys of the rich — the closed sedan overtook the open pleasure car in sales. People drove for business as well as recreation. Businessmen drove downtown, and their cars competed for parking space on the street; traffic signals came to Grand Rapids little by little; police learned to chalk the tires of cars parked too long; and more frequent crashes of streetcars and autos disturbed the peace. Jerry Ford, as the supervisor of traveling salesmen, had an automobile for work from early on; but all the other members of the Ford family "took the cars" (streetcars) downtown regularly on various errands until the end of the decade.

Downtown was, of course, the ceremonial center where the community came together to honor or celebrate on civic occasions. The largest in those years, the Grand Rapids centennial in September 1926, was observed with three days of parades and pageants. Junior Ford was among thousands of uniformed Boy Scouts who marched down Monroe Avenue in formation. The Christmas parade of the same year featured eighteen Scout troops, four floats, and several hundred Campfire Girls. All of the city's big churches were downtown, including St. Mark's Episcopal, where the Ford family by then

**The Fords'
church,
St. Mark's
Episcopal,
in the heart
of downtown**

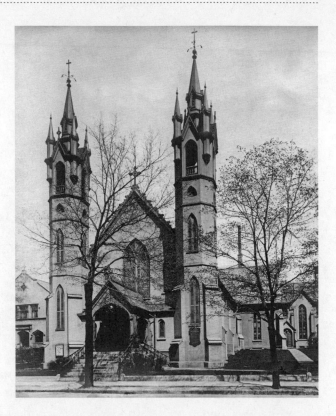

attended. A small stucco church with a pair of striking French Gothic spires, it was the church of many of the rich families from the Hill District.

Jerry and Junior swam nude in the modern pool at the newly built brick YMCA; in fact, this was where Junior learned to be an excellent swimmer, and he would eventually swim on the Y team. Junior practiced ballroom dancing at his Aunt Marjory's studio. His father's Elks Club, with its restaurant and bowling alley, was not far away. Jerry Sr. was active in the Elks, as he was in most business organizations, and in 1930 he served his turn as Grand Exalted Knight.

Across from the YMCA was the white-marble Ryerson Library, and only a few blocks away were the courthouse and city hall, both in the imposing castle-like style of the late 1800s. All told, it was a downtown to be proud of.

Overlooking downtown, the elegant mansions of the Hill District marked the beginning of the East Side, which ended two and a half miles farther east at the end of the streetcar line.

There, on Reeds Lake, the street railway company had built a popular amusement park, with roller-coaster rides, a fun house, a vaudeville theater, a pair of tiny double-decked steamboats that plied the lake, swimming at the bathing beach, and room for touring attractions such as balloon ascensions and parachute jumps. Every family in Grand Rapids knew about Ramona Park, which was by 1920 an established landmark, and many of them attended as often as they could in summer to enjoy the combination of woods, water, music, and carnival atmosphere. In the winter Reeds Lake froze and was used for ice skating. Daring motorists occasionally drove their vehicles out on the ice for fun, and every winter one or two ended up in the lake when the ice gave way unexpectedly.

Jerry and Dorothy Ford lived in one-half of 716-718 Madison Ave-

The Grand Rapids YMCA, where Junior Ford learned to swim

**College Avenue
in the Hill
District**

nue, with Jerry's mother and sister Marjory in the other half. That
neighborhood, south of the mansion area, was no longer upper-
class; one could call it the point where the East Side joined the South
Side, a working-class area much like the West Side except that men
worked more often for the railroads than in the furniture factories.
One of Jerry Ford's relatives, his nephew Harold Swain, managed a
coal company on the South Side near the railroad. Ethnically, the
area was a mixture: Syrian and Lebanese, Italian, Russian Jewish,
and a community of African-Americans who had moved to Grand
Rapids during World War I. But the largest group — numerous everywhere in the city but especially on the South Side — were the
Dutch immigrants, a clannish, industrious people who owned small
businesses or worked in clerical jobs and took their Protestant religion very seriously. To the rest of Michigan, Grand Rapids was a
Dutch city. It is almost ironically fitting that the young Jerry Ford,
blond, blue-eyed, open-faced — Dutch-looking but without a drop
of Dutch blood in him — would in maturity serve as this district's
representative in Congress.

As business improved after the post–World War I depression, Jerry Sr. saw his chance to get away from the fringes of the South Side. By that time, the far East Side of Grand Rapids, which had recently been incorporated as East Grand Rapids, the city's first suburb, was recognized as "the choice residential section of Grand Rapids," as one real estate advertisement in the 1920s put it. Lake Drive was its axis, bordered by large, often imposing houses and churches, punctuated occasionally by neighborhood commercial districts such as the one at the intersection of Lake Drive and Wealthy Street, with its café, shoestore, and drugstore, and the neighborhood theater affectionately known as Hinky Dink. It was in this developing area that Ford put down money to build a new

Reeds Lake at the Ramona Park landing in the 1930s

Junior Ford, second from bottom, with his cousins, the Swains, and Grandma Ford in the rear, 1921

house, the first he had ever owned, for himself, his wife, and his two sons, on Rosewood Avenue, a street that was just being laid out.

His nephew Harold Swain was about to build a home in the same area; the whole Ford clan seemed to be coming up in the world. A newly built house would have the modern conveniences that were coming to be important in the postwar world — electric wall outlets, kitchens and bathrooms with modern fixtures, and so on. Dorothy looked forward to entertaining there. They moved into the new house in 1922.

Unfortunately, they did not enjoy it long. In 1921, the owner of Heystek and Canfield had died, and his son, Harry Heystek Jr., took over the business. He began making management changes that were evidently not good choices, because the business folded entirely four years later. In 1923, Jerry Ford was one of the managers who lost his job. Briefly unemployed, he found work with a smaller company at a lower salary, but was unable to keep up the payments on the new house. "Well, I guess I'll just have to work harder," he told Dorothy as they were forced to move back into pre–World War I housing on the fringes of the Hill District.

This third home, which they rented at first and purchased two years later, was in the sloping 600 block of Union Avenue, in a typically mixed neighborhood for that part of the city.

Some residents owned, some rented; some were craftsmen, some owned their own businesses; one family was African-American; one family had a live-in maid. The majority of the homes were headed by men (or occasionally women) who were either from the low edge of the business class, such as salesmen, department store clerks, and stenographers, or the top of the working class, such as foremen and machinists. About half the families had originated in the Netherlands or were of Dutch extraction. The Fords' house, built in 1907, had two floors and a partially finished attic. It had a generous first-floor porch with removable screens, and upstairs there was a sleeping porch, a popular feature in the early twentieth century —

649 Union Avenue, Junior Ford's boyhood home

before air conditioning. The garage in back was a two-story stable from the horse-and-buggy era, now converted into a garage for the family car. Jerry Sr. kept his car in the lower level, and Junior and his buddies had surreptitious poker games in the upper story, reachable only by ladder. It was a good hideaway, Junior thought, because he figured that neither of his parents would venture up the ladder to find them. But Jerry Sr. was onto their gaming, and he caught them red-handed more than once — with the resulting "severe reprimand," as Ford put it in later years.

It was a neighborhood with a lot of children. As in most American towns of the time, those kids made the street their playground. On snowy days in winter, when driving was dangerous, the city would barricade Union Street hill, and they could coast down the street on their Flexible Flyers, or, in the case of the poorer families, homemade bobsleds. And all year long, they had the run of the neighbors' backyards.

Junior was almost ten when the family moved to 649 Union Avenue, and he spent almost all the rest of his school years in that house, which is officially recognized today as his boyhood home. For much of the week, he was the man of the house, because his father was traveling again, back on the road Monday through Friday for his new employer, the Grand Rapids Wood Finishing Company. This small firm, located on the far south side of the city, produced varnishes for the furniture business in an era when new specialty finishes were becoming popular. Its owner, Albert Simpson, was a fellow Mason and a personal friend. Jerry Ford was an excellent salesman — persistent, committed, pleasant, well-informed — the kind of man who made it a point of honor to stand behind the quality of his product. He made a good impression in his new job.

But Jerry Sr. was often away from home, and it fell to Junior — as his most responsible chore — to take care of the furnace. During the cold season, from October through April, he had to go down to the cellar every morning between six and six-thirty and spend half an hour shoveling yesterday's ashes out of the coal furnace and putting in a day's supply of coal, which lay loose in the coal bin. The heat produced by the furnace came upstairs via hot-air registers in the floor. There was a certain amount of technique associated with keeping a coal furnace burning evenly all day: variations in the draft, controlled in most households by a chain from upstairs, could make it burn fast or slow. All of that was Junior's responsibility. And every night, once he had learned the technique — probably when he was eleven or twelve — he banked the coal in the furnace so that it would burn evenly throughout the night.

Having a furnace and central heating put the Fords in the upper half of Grand Rapids' population in the 1920s. Probably 50 percent of the city's homes, including those of many of the Fords' neighbors, still had the heating systems of the previous age: gas heaters in the living room, dining room, and parlor, and no heat at all in the bedrooms. Some still heated their homes with coal or wood stoves (i.e., room stoves, not furnaces). On the other hand, families more wealthy than the Fords had automatic stokers that eliminated the need to adjust the draft and constantly add coal.

Junior was a hard worker, and like any oldest child, he felt honored to take on a share of his parents' adult roles. Good-humored and quiet, he took over many chores in his preteen and early teen years: sweeping the porch and mowing the lawn; emptying the drip pan under the icebox (electric refrigerators existed but were quite new and owned mostly by the rich); cooking basic meals for the family on the gas range when his mother was ill. This happened with some frequency in those years, as her added weight brought on a heart condition. When the two younger brothers, Dick and Jim, came along in 1924 and 1927 respectively, Junior was regularly responsible for changing their diapers for the same reason. On one occasion he kidded his mother that he had changed more diapers than she had.

Most of the time, of course, Dorothy was well and entertaining her guild or her bridge club, filling the prewar, unelectrified kitchen with rich smells. The small but attractive living room was dominated by her piano — she was the only family member who played — and by mementos of her New England ancestors. To the family, the most important location was the dining room, separated from the living room by sliding wooden "pocket doors," with the big round dining table, oak or mahogany according to whose version you believe, where family meals took place. One of Jerry Sr.'s three simple rules for his sons was: "Come to dinner on time." Occasionally, too, the parents had friends over for dinner. The boys were taught to clear the table and wash the dishes without being asked; indeed, they were trained to clear the table even when they were guests in other people's homes.

Dorothy had household help, the mark of a middle-class family, even when finances were tight. By the 1930s, when Jerry Sr. was part owner of a manufacturing company and the family lived in East Grand Rapids, they regularly had a maid. With her back problems and high blood pressure, Dorothy really needed help, particularly with heavy jobs such as laundry. And there were many young Dutch and German girls available. Moreover, she liked to entertain, and that preference gave her still more reason to hire a maid.

What did Dorothy Ford cook for her family? In the 1920s, when there were no frozen foods and only a few packaged or canned foods, cooking was from scratch. The Fords preferred the hearty old-fashioned breakfast of eggs and bacon, toast and coffee, which they consumed as Jerry Sr. read the front page and Junior got the sports section to check out the baseball scores. Most of the family members were gone for lunch, the older boys at school and Jerry on the road. Dinner was the big family meal, more formal than it would be today, with mashed potatoes, vegetables, and meat dishes. (Pot roast was Junior's favorite dinner.) Manners were strictly observed: a boy who put his elbow on the table was apt to have it thwacked with a spoon by his father. At dinner parents and sons shared their experiences of the day, always beginning with a prayer of blessing.

The second floor was where the small size of the house became most evident. The parents had one bedroom, and Junior and Tom shared the other — and then with Dick and Jim as they got old enough to leave their parents' side. The whole family shared one bathroom among them. It had the spare conveniences of the pre–World War I years: a toilet, a sink, and a bathtub — but no shower. In the 1920s showers were only for athletes and the rich.

By twenty-first-century standards, the Fords' life on Union Avenue seems limited and inconvenient. By the standards of Grand Rapids in the 1920s, it was about average, or a bit above average. There were many families on the side streets or alleys in their part of the city — African-American families and recently arrived Dutch im-

Albert H. Simpson, Jerry Ford Sr.'s boss and business partner

migrants in particular — who lacked a coal furnace or any kind of central heating, relying instead on the older technology of gas space heaters for each room. About half had no indoor plumbing; thus they still used backyard pit outhouses and got by with sponge baths. A considerable number had no electricity and no telephone. The Fords had one telephone, which was located near the front door at the foot of the stairs. When the caller needed a little privacy — which happened more frequently as Junior got into his teenage years — he closed the pocket doors of the living and dining rooms to create what the family called the "phone booth" at the bottom of the stairs.

Their life was fully as comfortable as that of most families living in Grand Rapids at the time. But Jerry Sr. dreamed of more. Over the next few years he moved in the direction of financial independence. He won the confidence of his boss, Albert Simpson, and convinced him that the firm ought to branch out into interior paints for use by the Dutch decorators and contractors who dominated the local market.

That made sense to Simpson. The furniture business in Grand Rapids had reached a plateau because of competition, particularly in the less expensive lines that were being produced in Southern states. From 1924 on, sales began slowing or dropping. There was good reason for a manufacturer of wood finishes to branch out a little, to have a second line of products as a hedge against the slump. Simpson, therefore, let Ford open a paint division, for which Simpson bought a small concrete-block factory building on the north side of the city, at the intersection of Crosby and Elizabeth streets, on the Pere Marquette Railroad line.

Simpson bought and installed grinders and mixers. Carl Schumann, a chemist who had just come to Grand Rapids from working for Pratt and Lambert in Minneapolis, came to work for Grand Rapids Wood Finishing with a couple of patents that might lead to a distinctive product. With Schumann as the technical director, and with Jerry Ford's contacts and sales ability, there might be a chance for a real profit. The operation began in February 1928.

IT'S NEW—

"DO"

DEODORIZED

PAINT

VARNISHES and ENAMELS

MASKING THE ODOR! No longer the Objectionable Turpentine "Smell" . . . an Exclusive Feature!

EVERYTHING FOR FINISHING WOOD, METAL, CONCRETE OR BRICK

FORD

PAINTS VARNISHES AND ENAMELS

A SATISFACTORY PRODUCT

FOR EVERY PURPOSE

FORD PAINT AND VARNISH CO.

MADE **RIGHT** IN GRAND RAPIDS

Over 3,000 homes and the majority of Grand Rapids' most prominent buildings have been decorated with "Ford's" *Better Paints, Varnishes and Enamels.*

Remember it is economy to have your decorating done by a Master Painter.

FORD PAINT AND VARNISH CO.

601-611 CROSBY, NW.

"Made RIGHT in Grand Rapids" was the Ford Paint and Varnish Company's slogan

The Ford Paint and Varnish factory

Thinking further, Simpson decided that he preferred to spin the paint operation off as a separate company if Ford and Schumann could raise the necessary cash. They could take over the management while continuing to use Simpson's plant and machinery, which they could purchase from him over time if the business fulfilled expectations. Undoubtedly Jerry Ford, anxious to become his own boss and earn the status he coveted, played a large part in this decision. He was confident that he could use his longtime sales experience to make the product sell. With Simpson committed to being the biggest investor, Jerry hustled out into the business community and found additional financial backing from local men who knew and trusted him. The new business, called Ford Paint and Varnish, began operations with $50,000 preferred stock, 2500 common shares with no par value, all subscribed and $25,000 paid in, a bookkeeper, and four employees in addition to Ford and Schumann. Its slogan emphasized both product quality and local origin: "Made *Right* in Grand Rapids!" It opened for business in October 1929.

October 1929 is an ill-omened month for Americans familiar with economic history: it was the month of the great stock-market crash that has always signaled, to later generations, the beginning of the Great Depression. At the time, however, it was not clear to most Americans what it signaled. By 1930 the federal government was acting vigorously, and the economy seemed to be recovering. Jerry Ford, intent on getting his business established and proud of his progress, wanted a new residence that would reflect his status as the head of his own business. He began looking for a new home in East Grand Rapids, and by the summer of 1930 he found what he was looking for: a large, white two-story wood-frame house at 2163 Lake Drive. Lake Drive was the main street that connected Grand Rapids' downtown and the Hill District with the East Side, and then, as it meandered toward Ramona Park, with East Grand Rapids itself. The house was of prewar construction, and it needed repair; but it had a den on the ground floor, four large bedrooms upstairs, and a generous lot. Jerry put money down on it, and every weekend that summer he and the family were over on Lake Drive sweeping, scraping, cleaning, and fixing up their new home. By September they had moved in.

The new house awed the boys with its size. Dick Ford remembers that the four brothers, aged three through seventeen, shared one enormous bedroom upstairs rather than dispersing. No doubt the whole family enjoyed the spacious yard and the proximity of Reeds Lake. But as 1931 began and the economic weather became stormier, Jerry Ford Sr. began to wonder if he had taken on more house than he could afford. This was the year Jerry Jr. was to graduate from high school, and as business conditions grew worse, college costs loomed ahead. Jerry Sr. had made it up the ladder of success and found even more challenges waiting at the top.

A young,
dressed-up
Junior Ford

3 Willingly to School

Kindergarten is something most Americans take for granted, but in the early twentieth century it was new — part of the bigger Progressive movement for reform and reorganization that was sweeping the country's schools. Grand Rapids had added kindergarten to its curriculum earlier than many other school systems. When little Junior Ford began school in 1918, he had ahead of him the chance for a superior public-school education. And he and his mother did not have far to go: they just had to walk down the block and across the street.

Fortress-like Madison School, a two-story brick structure with twelve classrooms, was the oldest building in the system, but it had an excellent reputation. The little boy, as he went from kindergarten through third grade, was probably not conscious of the quality teaching he was receiving, but he loved the school for another reason: it was near the city's Firehouse Number 7, the last station house in Grand Rapids where the engine was still drawn by a team of horses. When there was a fire, the alarm would scream, "the station house doors would swing open, and the teams of horses would come charging out," Ford said in later years. "The sight was spectacular."

After third grade, his father bought the new house on Rosewood,

Madison School and he attended school in East Grand Rapids for a year. For these first few years, Junior's temper tantrums, his stuttering, and his difficulty learning to write probably made him something of a problem student from his teachers' point of view. To Dorothy Ford, naturally, he was not a problem but a treasure, and she went about helping him succeed with the same untiring determination she applied to the rest of her life. She set up a time for his homework and insisted that he do it carefully and check it with her. She and her husband joined the Parent Teacher Association and took a large part in its activities. Jerry Sr. backed her up wholeheartedly. He always emphasized steady and honest effort, without slacking, to his sons. Neither

Dorothy nor Jerry believed in physical punishment, but they used all
the standard repertory of behavior modification: confinement, dep-
rivation of privileges, motivational talks. Junior did not need a lot of
discipline in any case; he was basically a cooperative boy.

Not much is known about Junior's fourth-grade year in East
Grand Rapids. In 1923 the family moved back to the near southeast
side of Grand Rapids, to Union Avenue, back in the Madison School
district, and Junior could walk the three blocks to school every

Ford's quite
legible hand-
writing as a
college junior

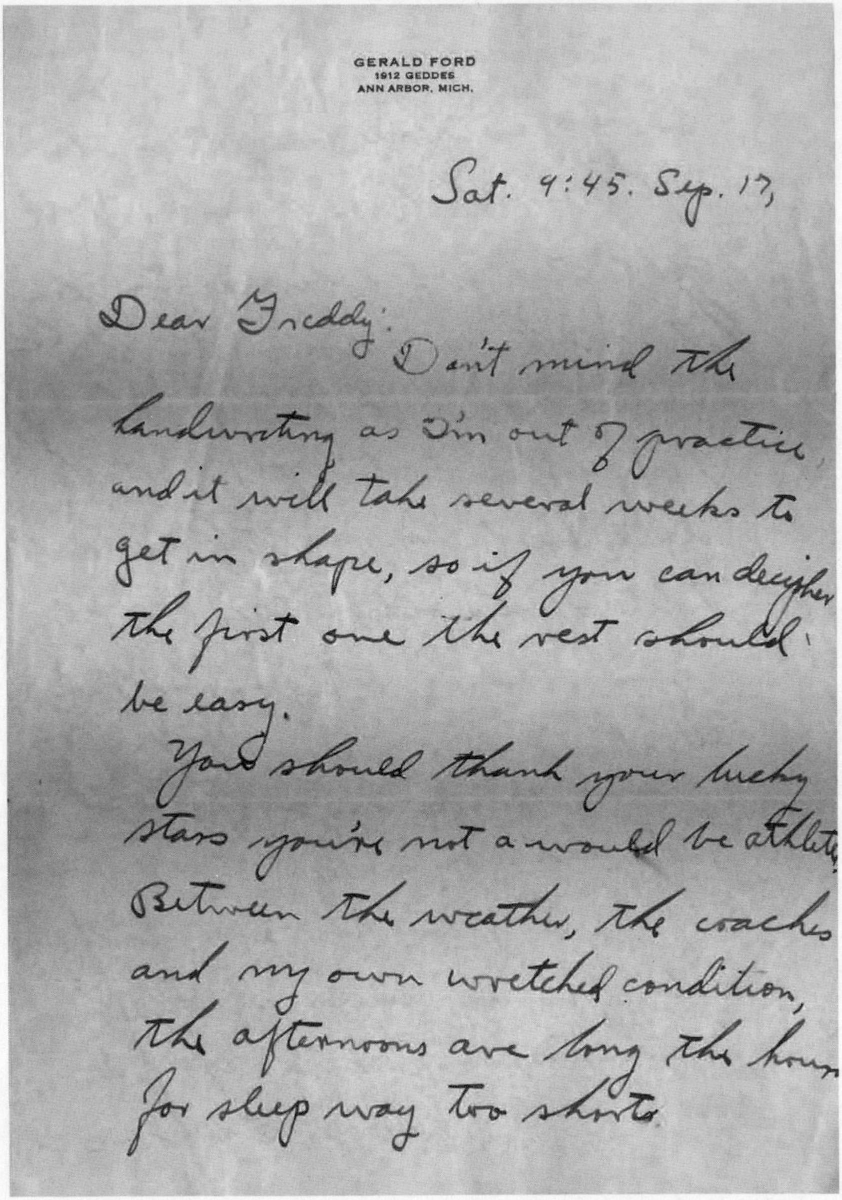

GERALD FORD
1912 GEDDES
ANN ARBOR, MICH.

Sat. 9:45. Sep. 17,

Dear Freddy:
                    Don't mind the
handwriting as I'm out of practice,
and it will take several weeks to
get in shape, so if you can decipher
the first one the rest should
be easy.
        You should thank your lucky
stars you're not a would be athlete.
Between the weather, the coaches
and my own wretched condition,
the afternoons are long the hours
for sleep way too short.

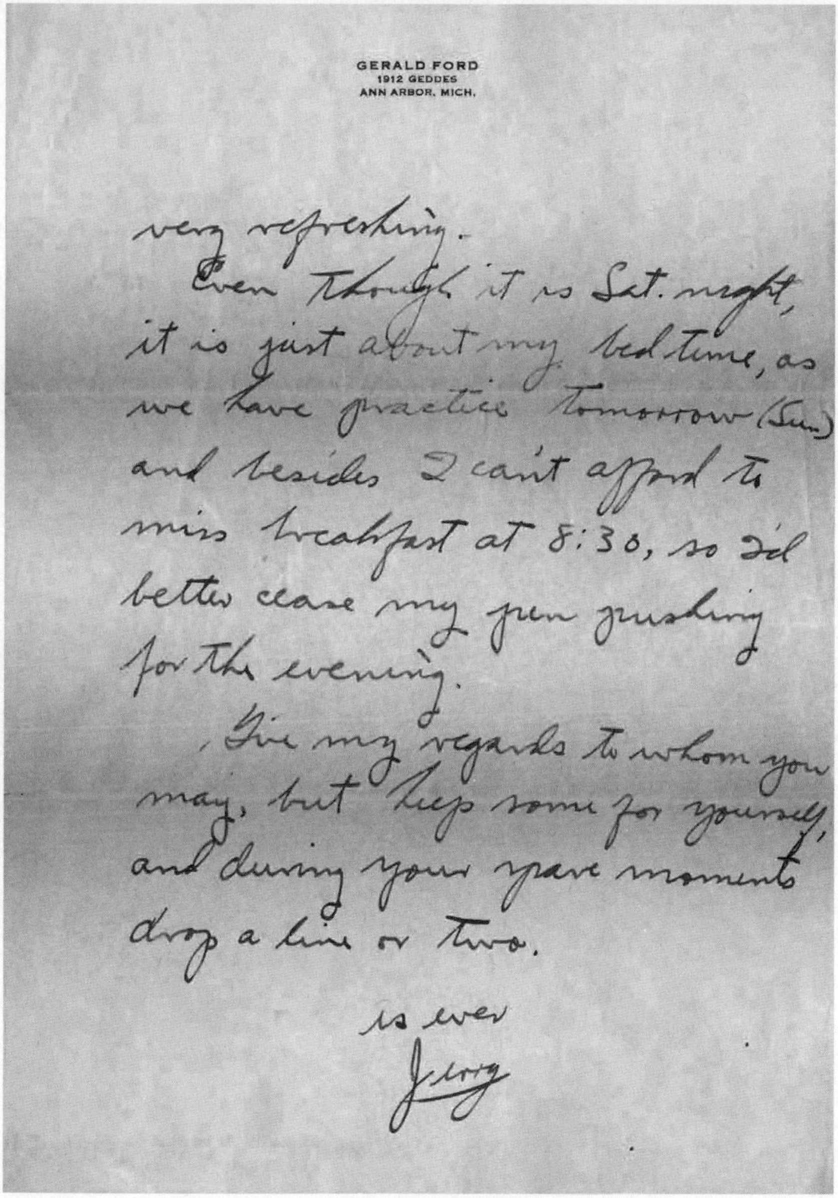

GERALD FORD
1912 GEDDES
ANN ARBOR, MICH.

very refreshing.

Even though it is Sat. night, it is just about my bed time, as we have practice tomorrow (Sun) and besides I can't afford to miss breakfast at 8:30, so I'd better cease my pen pushing for the evening.

Give my regards to whom you may, but keep some for yourself, and during your spare moments drop a line or two.

is ever

Jerry

Junior Ford with his mother and baby brother, Dick

morning, this time with his schoolmates. He made lots of friends in the Union Avenue neighborhood. The blond-haired Engle twins, Art and Ben, lived in a house on Paris Avenue whose back yard abutted the Fords' yard, and they became constant companions, romping across fences and through yards in standard schoolboy fashion. (Sylvia English, who lived on the block, recalled seeing Junior swinging from Georgia Hopper's clothesline pole.) In winter they were part of the gang that sledded down the Union Avenue slope to Franklin, when the city closed the streets to auto traffic. In summer they followed the ice wagon around, picking up chips to suck on or to put down girls' backs.

Burt Garel, another frequent companion, was African-American, the son of a chauffeur who lived on Bates Street. School mornings he would walk down Thomas Street to the corner of Union and Thomas and wait for Junior to join him. The two also hung around together in Madison Park after school, ice-skated on the rink, and

The Court of King Arthur, some of Junior Ford's childhood reading

played tag and pom-pom-pullaway with the other kids. Junior was stronger, but Burt was faster. Garel remembered how the girls had an interest in good-looking Junior, with his blond hair and blue eyes, but how his friend, tongue-tied, resolutely ignored them. Garel enjoyed visiting the Fords' house, not just because of the milk and cookies Mrs. Ford always offered him but because it felt to him, somehow, like a rich person's house. Maybe it was the piano.

When the neighborhood boys got together, at Madison Park or elsewhere, there were always games — unorganized games of base-ball and football. No Little League or any comparable organization existed at that time, and Jerry Ford Sr. worked too hard to take much part in his boys' sports, though he tossed a football with Junior now and then. Junior found out in these neighborhood games that he

South High School, 1929

would never be a baseball star: he was too slow. But he really enjoyed physical activity, and he was big. Football might be a possibility in time, he thought. Nor did he shy away from physical contact; he had his share of boyish fights. His last fistfight, which ended with a black eye for him and a bloody nose for his antagonist, is said to have taken place in fifth or sixth grade. In seventh or eighth grade he broke his collarbone, but no story survives to explain the circumstances.

Junior had indoor pastimes too, though those played a smaller part in his life. In addition to the poker games with the Engle twins, he worked on a stamp collection for a time.

His mother gave him a set of the Book of Knowledge children's encyclopedia and the tales of King Arthur and his knights. But Junior did not read many books, nor did anyone else in the house. One partial exception was the Horatio Alger books his father gave him to read. Those stories were obviously important to Jerry Sr. because they mirrored his own life and values. The point of those stories was not only that a poor boy could become prosperous by means of hard work, but that a poor boy could keep his moral values intact while becoming prosperous. Junior somehow sensed his father's esteem for them. These were the only books he remembered reading in bed.

Through fifth and sixth grade, with the good study habits he had internalized, Junior received above-average grades. By this time, his younger brothers were starting to become factors in his life. For example, when he sold magazines around the neighborhood, seven-year-old Tom pulled the wagon. But the younger brothers never interfered with his studying, even when they were playing in the same room. Junior had a remarkable ability to focus on whatever he was doing and block out everything else. His parents' efforts had paid off.

Madison School had only six grades. After sixth grade — for seventh and eighth grades, ordinarily called junior high or middle school today — students went to the relatively new South High School (built in 1916) on the corner of Jefferson Avenue and Hall Street, four blocks farther south and four to the west.

South High was a typical early twentieth-century high school: a three-story brick building with large windows, with separate wings for the junior-high classes and the older students. It was within walking distance of the Ford home on Union Avenue (slightly more than a mile), but a good deal longer walk than to Madison School. Almost the same distance to the northwest, in the Hill District, stood Central High School, the old, established, prestigious high school of the city, where Jerry Sr.'s old friend Ralph Conger was the basketball coach. With a little help from influential friends, it would be easy to get Junior enrolled at Central, where he would make personal friendships with the sons and daughter of the Grand Rapids upper class. The idea interested Junior's father enough to talk it over with Coach Conger.

The pros and cons were hard to assess: the two schools were about the same distance away, but most of Junior's friends from the neighborhood would be going to South, not Central. Both schools had fairly modern facilities, though South was newer by a few years. Both had excellent principals and first-class faculties. On the other hand, Central drew its students from the families of mill owners, lawyers, and civic leaders, while South students' parents were likely to be railroad workers, small business owners, mechanics, and even farmers who sent their kids to the city for school.

"You send Junior to South," Conger said. "That's where he'll learn more about living."

Conger may have had another point in the back of his mind, though there is no record that he expressed it. What would the experience be like from Junior's standpoint? If he went to Central, the Ford family's moderate resources would not allow him to keep up with the social style of the rich kids who ran the school. He could get lost in the shuffle or find his high school years a continual experience of frustration. At South, on the other hand, his family's financial position would allow him to stand out and to be a student leader himself. Ford himself, toward the end of his life, looked at the choice from that angle:

"That advice to go to South was a critical decision," he told an interviewer. "If I had gone to Central, I probably would have been one of those smartass" — he broke off and rephrased the thought: "In the first place, I could not afford to do the things that most kids did there." Whatever the reason, Jerry and Dorothy Ford, after full consideration, chose to send their son to South, where he would become fully acquainted with the mixed population of the South Side.

So Junior Ford found himself in September 1925 in a cavernous "session room" (homeroom), seated with eighty-odd other students, two by two, in rows of wooden desks. The scale of the place was intimidating, with its high ceilings, tall windows, long corridors, and many staircases. So was the rush of feet during the change of classes, when the bigger kids, the teenagers (though that word was not yet in use), burst out of their classrooms. It was easy to get lost, and easier to feel lost, especially for kids from small schools on the far South Side. Two gymnasiums, one for boys and one for girls, a cafeteria, a community room, a band room, a chorus room, and an auto shop — all made for a complexity unknown in primary school. The library was large, and in the high-school part of the school com-

Arthur W. Krause, the principal of South High

51

plex, reproductions of classic sculpture — Joan of Arc and the discus thrower, among others — were strategically placed around the halls.

The environs of the school were a new kind of neighborhood for Junior and many other seventh-graders. South stood near the middle of Grand Rapids' Little Italy, right across from Our Lady of Sorrows Church, where, on feast days, men in suits came out and carried giant crosses or statues in processions. Italian groceries and businesses lined Hall Street to the west. On the corner of Jefferson was the railway company's big car barn for all the streetcars in the system. The main railroad line was only a few blocks away, and there were constant toots, wails, and blasts from locomotive engines. Around the school were a couple of small businesses that were student hangouts, where the bigger kids would spend lunch break. School buses were not a feature of the scene — they were not in use yet — and cars were few. Almost all students walked to school, many from much farther than Junior had to walk, wrapped in caps and overcoats against the winter weather.

As they became integrated into the school, the seventh- and eighth-graders heard tales of the teachers, mysterious semimythological beings who could have an impact on their future.

Mr. Krause, the principal, was a short, trim, serious man, reputed to be tough but fair. Miss Linsley, the bubbly chorus teacher, was a miracle worker who could teach any student to sing and whose choruses always placed high in competitions. Round, smiling Mr. Wickett, who taught algebra, was liked for his interest in sports and his propensity to spend the whole class period talking about last week's game. On the other hand, students were intimidated by the harelipped librarian who was always shushing people and by Mr. LeValley, a lean World War I veteran who taught business and enforced iron discipline with a ruler, pausing now and then to share his wartime experiences. There was the beautiful, otherworldly art teacher, Miss Vevia, who seemed to exist on another planet but helped some students to use talents they never suspected they had.

In the seventh grade, and again in the tenth, Junior studied English under Lucy Reed, a well-liked, cheerful teacher in Room 311. Her grade books have survived, and that fact allows a later generation to follow Ford's performance in detail as he took tests on participles and prepositions, read books and wrote themes, memorized Emerson's "Concord Hymn" and Milton's "On His Blindness." He was never at or near the head of the class, but almost always in the middle, whatever the assignment was. Miss Reed's verdict on him in later years contained words of high praise from a teacher: he was "quiet" and "always prepared." He was the kind of student a teacher liked to have in class.

A class like Miss Reed's, with clear rules and recognition of students who did their assigned work, was the kind of educational experience Junior enjoyed most. The pleasure he took in structured learning was again evident in his class in modern history, which he enrolled in for his junior year. He was one of the two best students in the class; the other was a fifteen-year-old sophomore, Virginia Berry, who was taking extra courses in order to graduate early.

"Our teacher gave weekly exams," she remembered later, "and the way it went was, one week I would get a ninety-six and Jerry a ninety-three, next week he'd get a ninety-seven and I'd get a ninety-four. I sat in the back of the room and Jerry up front, and every time exams were returned he would come back to ask what my grade was. He didn't resent it if I got a better grade; he was just checking. We both got A's in that subject, the only two in the class."

It is worth noting that young Ford, whose performance in English was fairly average, was regularly at the top of the class in history — not only in that class, but in most of the history courses he took. His classmates noticed it early on, and by high school they used to enjoy getting him to speak up and deliver his opinions in history classes. The reason for his interest seems obvious: young Ford deeply respected his stepfather, and at home — around the dinner table and elsewhere — he often heard Jerry Sr. talk about social problems in the community, or the nation, or the world. Fortified by his father's opinions, he was confident in stating them to other people, and interested in classes where such questions were studied. It was a surprising contrast to his usual silence.

In the Grand Rapids school system, when most students were at the end of eighth grade and had reached the age of fourteen, they had finished the limit of compulsory education in Michigan. At that point, a large portion of the class, perhaps 40 percent, dropped out to take jobs in the adult world (such as Junior's friend Burt Garel). Those who remained had to decide what they were in high school to achieve: a general education, with an emphasis on business skills like typing and mechanical drawing, or an academic education, with the prospect of college. The academic group was the smaller group of those who stayed in high school. In eighth grade, then, students and their parents had to decide whether college might be a possibility.

Jerry Sr., one of those who had been forced to leave high school after the eighth grade, was eager to see Jerry Jr., the son he had come to think of as his own, go on to college, though it would cost a lot and scholarships were few. The achievement would validate his own success in the business world as well as give the boy a chance at a bright future. Junior was aware of his father's eagerness. The only question was what direction his studies should take when he got to a college, since most jobs did not yet require a college degree, and the range of programs in higher education was relatively narrow. At some point during his eighth-grade year, Junior surprised his parents by announcing that he wanted to study law. It was a surprising choice in some ways. There were no lawyers in the Ford family, or among their close friends, so the profession was an unknown country. Of course, it was respectable and promised a good income. But for a quiet boy who still had trouble speaking in public, becoming an attorney, with its emphasis on verbal performance, did not seem like a natural fit.

Junior did not try to explain what led him to choose law, but from his career it is obvious that neither big money nor fame as a speaker and writer was his goal. Probably his motivation lay in those dinner-table conversations with his father. From them he got the understanding that society, like the family and the school, is governed by rules; that the rules are for the purpose of helping people lead successful lives; and that problems arise at all levels of society when rules are disregarded. Lawyers, by definition, were people who understood those rules and made sure they were observed correctly. To be a lawyer was to do something self-evidently worthy. If verbal skill was a requirement, he would somehow acquire enough of that to get by.

The road to the bar examination was long — and not cheap: four years of the college-preparatory course in high school, four undergraduate years in some college, and a couple more years at a law school. But his parents had promised moral and financial support, and he would give it his best effort. When the time came to fill out his ninth-grade schedule, he chose algebra and first-year Latin, and he nerved himself for the challenges ahead.

Eagle Scout
Jerry Ford and
a friend at Fort
Mackinac

4 Playing by the Rules

Jerry and Dorothy Ford did an impressive job of inspiring their oldest son to believe in a kind, fair, ordered society, but they had powerful help from Grand Rapids itself. It was a city where morality was very important, partly because its churches were so strong. To the rest of Michigan it had a reputation for piety, a kind of "conspicuous Christianity" — at least to some Grand Rapids citizens who did not share it. One of them, Dorothy Judd, called the city "remarkably conservative" in religious matters; "straitlaced" was Gerald Ford Jr.'s own characterization years later. "Little Jerusalem!" exclaimed a physician from Ann Arbor in 1930. "Everywhere you look in Grand Rapids, you see a church. They fill them up Sunday morning, Sunday evening, prayer meeting in the middle of the week. You're always praying for something over there in Grand Rapids. . . ." The *Grand Rapids Herald,* one of the two major dailies, carried a Bible verse every day on its editorial page and was squeamish in its coverage of moral offenses. The *Grand Rapids Press,* the other daily, did not even publish on Sundays.

The city's reputation contrasted sharply with that of Detroit, the high-living boomtown on the other side of the state. When a Grand Rapids man told a group of friends how the street railway company had run an "owl" streetcar fifteen minutes after midnight on New

Year's Eve so that downtown revelers could get home, a Detroiter laughed and said that in his city the parties were just starting at that hour.

Everyone in Grand Rapids was aware of the two Dutch Calvinist churches, the Reformed Church and the even stricter Christian Reformed Church, with its prohibition of all dancing, the cinema, and premarital sex. Their energetic disputes about how serious a sin it was to attend a baseball game on Sunday or a movie under any circumstances amazed and amused the rest of the city. But there was also a strong, vigorous Catholic community; a rescue mission and a Salvation Army deeply involved in helping the poor; fervent groups like the Pentecostals, Spiritualists, and Assemblies of God; and, of course, the mainline denominations, Congregationalists, Presbyterians, Methodists, American Baptists, each with an imposing building in a downtown location.

The Fords were Episcopalians, and they attended St. Mark's Church on Division Avenue in the heart of town. They found spiritual nourishment in the elaborate ritual and the sonorous words of the Book of Common Prayer ("Almighty God, Father of our Lord Jesus Christ, maker of all things, judge of all men, we acknowledge and bewail our manifold sins and wickedness . . ."). A study of Michigan Episcopalians written in the 1930s contains a description of the "typical Episcopalian" that could have been written to describe any of the Fords. It used the masculine pronoun, in the style of the time, but meant both sexes: a typical Episcopalian "will be found to have a marked sense of law and order, of reverence for God and respect for sacred places and persons, to be liberal in matters which he regards as non-moral, to value education and demand truth. He dislikes emotional excesses in religion, which he regards as a personal matter, and he stands for respectability and good manners."

The rule of the Episcopal Church at that time was that a divorced person who remarried was in a state of sin. Dorothy Ford, therefore, was ineligible for communion, and the family did not formally join the church; but they attended regularly and had the full respect of their fellow churchgoers.

The rich families of the Hill District who attended church at St. Mark's tended to take their Christianity seriously, and they sponsored civic groups to beautify the city or to help the sick and the poor. In the words of a son of Grand Rapids a generation younger than Ford: "Rich people in Grand Rapids, unless they have some enormous pile of inherited loot, so big it takes them two quarts of gin a day to stay on top of it, unless they are in these extremities they tend to go in for some kind of civic enterprise." They were serious, too, about observing the law. The 1920s were the heart of the Prohibition era, when in many cities, such as gangster-ridden Detroit, the law against drinking was openly and proudly violated. In Grand Rapids the upper class observed Prohibition. Many remembered the society wedding between two leading families of the Hill District at which the guests toasted the bride and groom not with champagne but with cold water. There was no secret liquor cabinet in the Ford home either, and Dorothy made all her sons promise not to smoke or drink until they were grown.

All this is not to say that Grand Rapids was populated by angels: like any other city, it had liquor raids, prostitution, and a skid row. The point is that, in Grand Rapids, the upper class was conspicuously on the side of moral behavior. For a man like Jerry Ford Sr., who wanted to belong to that class, morality was not only the right thing to do; it was also a social and business advantage. "Grand Rapids," in the words of a local newspaperman, "was a town that rewarded virtue."

Junior Ford could see both his parents busy trying to improve the community. His father belonged to several organizations, but probably his favorite was the Youth Commonwealth, which he had helped to found. It was an organization that was founded to provide support and education for boys from poor families in rundown areas of the city. Its base of operations was on the South Side, actually not far from South High School, and Jerry put in so much time on it that Dorothy is supposed to have remarked that if he would spend that much time on his job, the family would be rich. But she had her own organizations: at Christmastime, for instance, she worked with the Santa Claus Girls, middle-class women who were organized to make and distribute gifts to poor families all over Grand Rapids.

Jerry Ford had long been deeply devoted to Masonry, the network of men's organizations that promoted personal development, honesty, philanthropy, and brotherhood among its members. His lodge, Malta, met Friday nights at the large, modern multistory temple downtown. The Fords frequently had some of those lodge brothers and their wives over for dinner, and they shared other social events. During the 1920s his involvement deepened, as he became affiliated with the Scottish Rite, a branch of Masons that emphasized getting the group's message across through drama and pageantry. Because of his stature and impressive physical presence, he was a natural performer. He had "the straightest shoulders of any man I ever knew," recalled his stepson.

A similar organization at the youth level was the Boy Scouts of America, still a new and growing organization in the 1920s, especially popular in towns and smaller cities like Grand Rapids. Its mission was to build character in American boys by means of outdoor activity and the challenge of a simulated wilderness environment under the guidance of a benevolent adult male. There were forty or fifty troops in Grand Rapids, and naturally Jerry Sr. was involved. His schedule on the road did not allow him to be a scoutmaster, but he served on various central committees; and Junior, long before he turned twelve and became eligible, was eager to become a Boy Scout. (The Cub Scouts had not yet been created; that happened in 1930.)

Junior's Scouting experience began in December 1925, and it was everything he anticipated. He loved being a Scout and was proud of it all his life — of that there is no doubt. But he rarely spoke about specific experiences, and fellow Scouts who knew him had few or no tales to tell about him. His career in the Scouts, consequently, has to be traced in terms of the ranks he earned and the awards he received. Behind the bland, impersonal records one has to imagine the fresh, goofy, exhilarating stories of a kid roaring through puberty, gaining height and weight every month until, at the end of his Scouting years, he stood six feet tall and weighed 140 pounds.

His first scoutmaster, Charles Kindel, was a young married man, heir to one of the big furniture factories in the city, and himself an Eagle Scout. To him, Junior swore the Scout Promise: "On my honor I will do my best to do my duty to God and my country and to obey the Scout Law; to help other people at all times; and to keep myself physically strong, mentally awake, and morally straight."

Meeting every week with twenty or thirty East Side boys from twelve to fifteen, he began the round of games, physical activities, and outdoor camping that would help him advance step by step in rank. Scouting, with its exercise, inspirational message, and clear rules, suited Junior perfectly. He persuaded half a dozen of his Union Avenue buddies, the Engle twins and others, to join the troop. Together, they formed a patrol, and they elected Junior their leader.

Through the winter and spring Troop 15 had its weekly meetings, occasional camping excursions, and participation in public functions and parades like the great Grand Rapids Centennial in 1926. They turned out with other troops to take part in citywide projects for beautification and getting out the vote. But the centerpiece of the year for them, as it was for most Scouts, was summer camp, where the troop camped together, swam and learned archery, hiked and rowed or sailed boats, learned about woodland creatures and nature, and passed all the tests of skill and memory that were required to advance in rank and earn merit badges.

Camp Shawondossee, named for the spirit of the South Wind from the *Song of Hiawatha,* was a primitive location in the woods near Lake Michigan, and Junior attended it during the summers of 1926 and 1927. The following year it was moved north of Muskegon

Part of the
Scout Law,
from the 1927
Boy Scouts of
America
Handbook

1. A SCOUT IS TRUST-WORTHY

A Scout's honor is to be trusted. If he were to violate his honor by telling a lie, or by cheating, or by not doing exactly a given task, when trusted on his honor, he may be directed to hand over his Scout Badge.

2. A SCOUT IS LOYAL

He is loyal to all to whom loyalty is due, his Scout leader, his home, and parents and country.

3. A SCOUT IS HELPFUL

He must be prepared at any time to save life, help injured persons, and share the home duties. He must do at least one "Good Turn" to somebody every day.

4. A SCOUT IS FRIENDLY

He is a friend to all and a brother to every other Scout.

5. A SCOUT IS COURTEOUS

He is polite to all, especially to women, children, old people and the weak and helpless. He must not take pay for being helpful or courteous.

6. A SCOUT IS KIND

He is a friend to animals. He will not kill nor hurt any living creature needlessly, but will strive to save and protect all harmless life.

The Scout uniform, from the 1927 Handbook

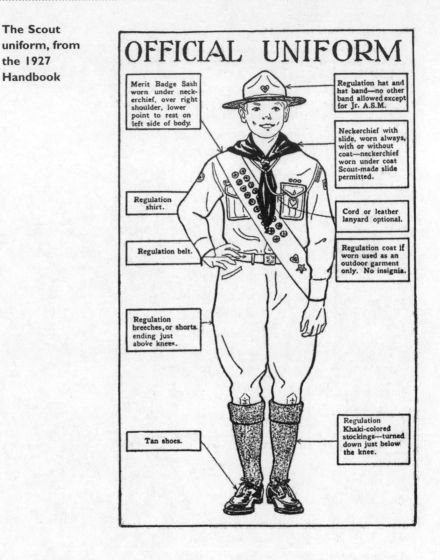

(present Duck Lake State Park) to a site with new buildings and much improved facilities. Indian lore was a central theme of camp activities, and the camp had a Menominee tribal member on its staff.

Young Ford's merit badge certificates chart his progress through the Scouts, an achievement he enjoyed. The process was congenial to his style of learning: it had definite rules, a demon-

SCOUT BADGES AND INSIGNIA

Tenderfoot · First Class · Star Scout
Second Class · First Class · Life Scout · Eagle Scout
Patrol Medallion · Community Strip · Troop Numeral · Service Star
Five Year Veteran · Ten Year Veteran · Fifteen Year Veteran · Twenty Year Veteran · Twenty Five Year Veteran
Assistant Patrol Leader · Patrol Leader · Senior Patrol Leader · Junior Assistant Scoutmaster
Achievement · Harmon Pin · Honor Medal for Life Saving
Sea Scout · Life Guard · Long Cruise Badge · Cabin Boy
Scribe · Bugler · Troop Quartermaster

Scout badges
and insignia,
from the 1927
Handbook

stration that generally contained physical activity, and a public reward. His first badges were for cooking and firemanship, which he earned on the troop's camping expeditions with Scoutmaster Kindel in the woods just beyond town. (He already knew cooking and tending a furnace from his responsibilities at home.) The first summer at camp, he qualified in swimming, athletics, first aid, and a variety of crafts. The following summer he earned thirteen

65

A group picture at camp, 1927; Ford is on left, at rear, in front of the tent door.

badges in all: lifesaving and physical development, which were easy for him; but also more specialized skills, such as carpentry and blacksmithing; and areas that required study, such as civics and scholarship. Each one was a step on the road to the highest rank a Scout could attain, that of Eagle Scout, which he reached on August 2, 1927, at the end of his second summer at Shawondossee. He was fourteen years old.

When he went back to camp for the summer of 1928, it was not as a camper but as a staffer, and he had a new name: in Scout records for that year he appears as Jerry Ford, or Gerald Jr. — no longer "Junior." He still belonged to troop 15, and he racked up a few more merit badges, but as an Eagle Scout he had reached the pinnacle. He was a member of the honor guard at the dedication of the new Camp Shawondossee. With the other staffers, he learned to perform Indian dances and war whoops for the weekly pageants.

A role model for the younger boys at camp, who admired his seriousness and sincerity — in a word, his character — he had become a very visible figure, with his tousled blond hair, which he made a point of wearing as uncombed as possible, and also his size: as one of the other scouts remembered him, he was a "big kid." As a model Boy Scout, he was singled out for all sorts of distinctions, including trips to other locations to represent his troop. As a staffer, he arrived

at camp early to help set up tents, make needed repairs, and kill rat-
tlesnakes before the younger boys got there.

Boy Scout records make it possible to date precisely when Junior
Ford began calling himself "Jerry," like his stepfather. It was in his
ninth-grade year, by the summer of 1928, when he turned fifteen.
But those Scout records cannot tell *why* he made the change. Certainly it was appropriate to his physical size and the leadership posi-

**Bob Slack of the
camp staff at his
tent in the
1930s**

tion he was coming to have in the Scouts that he no longer be known as "Junior." But it also reflected the increasingly close bond he was coming to feel with his stepfather: "Jerry" was a name of honor to him. Boyhood friends, with an effort, adapted little by little to calling him "Jerry" rather than "Junior." His mother never did; to her he was "Junior" all his life.

In the same year, ninth grade, he acquired another nickname. That was the year he began playing second-team football, and his teammates were boys who had known him as "Junior" through their years in school up to that point. Those teammates came up with a compromise between his old name and the new one he had just assumed: they called him "Junie." His athletic nickname became Junie Ford for the next three years at South High, originally among the players, then among the coaches as well. By his senior year, the rest of the school had learned it, and even Arthur Krause, the serious, businesslike principal, called him Junie on occasion. But that nickname failed to make it into Scout records, where from 1928 on he was "Jerry."

He was happy to get back to Shawandossee for six weeks on the staff in the summer of 1929, the summer he turned sixteen. Putting Scout values and attitudes into practice in an open-air setting dedicated to wholesome activity was as satisfying to him as ever. That summer he joined the Sea Scouts and helped sail a 72-foot schooner out onto Lake Michigan. As camp was about to close that year, he received from his adult leaders on the Grand Rapids Area Council an invitation that led to the climax of his summer, and perhaps of his entire adolescent Scouting experience.

Mackinac (pronounced "Mackinaw") Island, the fabulous limestone island in the straits between Lake Huron and Lake Michigan, which had become a summer playground for the rich families of the Midwest, was also home to a historic U.S. Army fort that was more than a century old. The federal government had donated Fort Mackinac to the state of Michigan to be a state park after it was taken out of active service in about 1900; but since then the fort had

Aerial view of the harbor at Mackinac Island with St. Ignace and the Upper Peninsula in the distance

been only indifferently maintained. It consisted of barracks, block houses, a few cannon, and a small museum located in a commanding position on the island. Summer visitors wandered through it as though exploring an interesting ruin. In 1929 a Scouting enthusiast on the state park commission had an inspiration: the state should assemble a small group of Eagle Scouts from every part of Michigan to serve as an "honor guard" that could present the fort's history to visitors, while simultaneously representing the best of present-day Michigan youth.

The whole opportunity came up quite suddenly, and the Grand Rapids council, pressed to choose their best Eagle Scout, quickly named Jerry Ford. So, at the beginning of August, instead of going back to work at Bill's and preparing for the fall football season, he donned his Scout uniform and was whisked off to Lansing to meet the other members of the Michigan honor guard, to have a picture taken with Governor Fred Green — then on to Detroit for more publicity.

The Eagle Scout Honor Guard with Governor Fred H. Green; Ford is in the second row

That night he found himself on a Great Lakes steamship, a side-wheeler, for the overnight voyage to Mackinac Island, which was (and remains) accessible only by water. No bridge connects it to the mainland, and no autos are permitted on the island.

The eight Eagle Scouts spent the month of August at Mackinac camped in the fort, cooking their own meals, and looking across at the Grand Hotel with its modern swimming pool, costumed employees, and two golf courses. Snappy in their uniforms, they gave tours of the fort, working in four-hour shifts. At sunset they fired the fort's cannon. When off duty, they were free to enjoy the delights of the "Cool Beauty Spot of the World" — the dramatic rock formations, the icy lake waters, the horse-drawn carriages, and the mag-

70

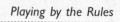

**Lake steamer
en route to
Mackinac;
Ford at left**

nificent views across the water. Most of them had cameras and recorded a series of breathtaking snapshots. Some arranged dates with girls staying at the hotel or the cottages, but Jerry abstained.

That whole month he had football on his mind. The upcoming season, as a later chapter will show, was important for the South High team and for him personally. Every morning at reveille he was up running laps around the fort, trying to stay in shape for football practice. He brought a ball along, and when he found another Eagle Scout, Joe McIntosh of Port Huron, who played center on his team, as Jerry did on South's team, he hung around with him in all his free time, and they worked on snapping the ball. His service at the fort on Mackinac Island in 1929 was effective, and it helped start a tradition that continues to the present. But it belonged to a part of Jerry's life that was now waning. Scouting had seen him through puberty; now team sports would be the center of his life for the next ten years. When he returned home in September, he wrote a nice thank-you

Relaxing with fellow scouts at Mackinac

letter to the State Park Commission and then turned to the business of the fall.

Eagle Scout Honor Guard in front of Fort Mackinac

But Ford's connection with Scouting and its ideals never ended. All his life he proudly acknowledged his close connection with Scouting, and Boy Scouts played a central part in his funeral ceremonies. At various times in his political career he was called a "Boy Scout" — sometimes admiringly, sometimes derisively. But those who used that term, whether friends or foes, were talking about the same qualities: it was a sense that, regardless of circumstances, he was trying to live up to a definite code of personal conduct and human relationships that he knew from Troop 15 and Camp Shawondossee. It was an attitude he already knew from his parents and the church, but Scouting expressed it in simple, definitive form: A Scout is trustworthy, a Scout is loyal, a Scout is helpful . . . it is the Scout Law.

YMCA swim team, 1931; Ford at far left

5 Friends and Fun

Mackinac Island had been a thrill, but Great Lakes adventure was already somewhat familiar to young Jerry Ford. He could remember beach vacations as far back as his preschool years. Almost all of them had been on Lake Michigan, with its white dunes on the shore and cold blue waveless water stretching to the western horizon. When he was small, the big lake was a convenient place for his family to meet the relatives from Chicago — Uncle Jim, Aunt Tannisse, and their children. Cousin Gardie James was nearly his own age; they were mates on the beach and in the water, as snapshots show. They spent time at different beaches on the lakeshore, fishing from docks or splashing in the water.

Jerry remembered learning to swim very early, and he swam constantly from then on, at the beach and at the YMCA. In his senior year in high school he would compete on the Y swimming team.

Ottawa Beach was the place to which the Ford family always returned. It was convenient to Grand Rapids, only thirty miles southwest by a good road, just north of an inlet that led from Lake Michigan to Black Lake (now Lake Macatawa) and the little town of Holland. Many of the affluent Grand Rapids folks owned cottages near the beach. In those years, the cottages looked out directly on the water instead of being separated from it by a huge dune, as they are now. A

Junior and his parents at Ottawa Beach with Uncle Jim James, about 1923

brisk west wind off the lake would blow beach sand into their front rooms. There was a rather grand resort hotel (until it burned down in 1923) that catered to vacationers from Chicago, who made the trip via a regular steamboat service of many years' standing. Some Chicagoans owned cottages there. Imposing side-wheelers of the Chicago & Holland line, as well as lake freighters, traversed the waters of Black Lake. South of the inlet there was another beach, called Macatawa.

Ottawa Beach cottages were not cheap, and Jerry Sr. and Dorothy did not own one until the late 1930s. Yet they managed to rent there or stay with friends almost every summer, quite often with Ralph Conger, the Central High School athletic director. "Uncle Ralph" and "Aunt Julia" and their son Gilbert figured in a lot of Ford family snapshots, playing on the beach or in the water with the line of cottages in the background. All the early photos showed the men and boys wearing two-piece swimsuits, with longish trunks and tank tops. It was not considered respectable for males to appear barechested until the 1930s.

To young Jerry Ford, as to many Grand Rapids people of his generation, Ottawa Beach held the fascination of an alternate world only a couple of hours from the Fords' front door. One walked across the dunes and entered a world of freedom and natural beauty — without obligations. For smaller kids it offered unlimited playtime, for teenagers, freedom to experiment with adult activities. The friends he made at Ottawa Beach, though they were from Grand Rapids, were not his South High or Union Avenue friends, but a different group of people. The impressions this time left on him lasted into later life, so much so that his postpresidential office in Grand Rapids was dominated by a painting of the sun setting over Lake Michigan.

A different kind of summer experience was the fishing camp near Bitely, some two hours north of Grand Rapids, that Jerry Sr. began visiting in 1924. This part of western Michigan — Newaygo and Lake Counties — abounds in dark, slow-flowing streams that empty into Lake Michigan, all with superb trout fishing. Grand Rapids businessmen made it an important part of their lifestyle to own a clubhouse or a cabin on one of the rivers and offer hospitality to friends. Some of these getaways were quite elaborate, with amenities and servants; others were more primitive. The region was known as the "Stump Country," because it had been completely cut over during the logging boom of the late 1800s, and its vistas consisted of stumps and scrawny alder and maple saplings, except next to the rivers, where there were some large trees left. In 1926, Jerry Sr. and five friends, all of them salesmen, joined together to purchase a cabin on the Little South Branch of the Pere Marquette River.

The cabin was primitive: a long, rambling building of logs chinked with cement, with a screened-in porch and stone chimney. It had no electricity or plumbing, and it could be reached only by traversing a couple of miles of dirt road. But its location on the trout stream was what counted. Snapshots show Jerry and other men out in the river in waders, fishing. Sometimes the whole family came up, and at least a couple of times they invited Leigh Nichols and his fam-

Grand Rapids Herald cartoonist Ray Barnes's 1934 map of Grand Rapidians' favorite fishing camps; Jerry Ford's fish camp, kiddingly labeled "Henry Ford," is at lower right

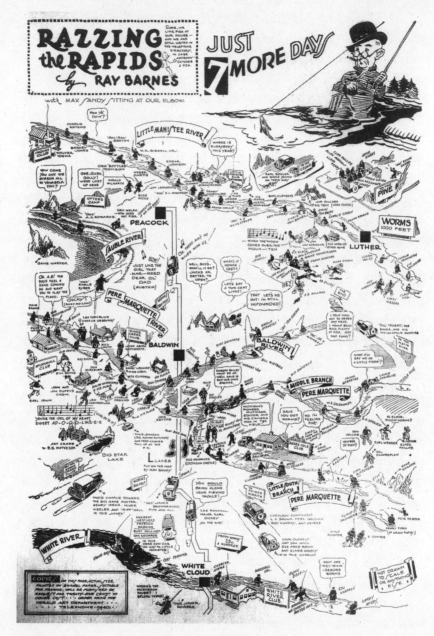

ily, their neighbors across Union Avenue. Nichols was a buyer at a department store downtown. He and his wife had three children who were close in age to the Ford boys.

A photo shows members of both families out on the river in a canoe with Junior paddling at the bow. Evidently, then, he knew how to manage a boat by the time he joined the Boy Scouts. Other cabins or fishing camps are remotely visible downriver, and there probably was a certain amount of visiting back and forth. But since they shared the use of the cabin with five other families, the Fords were up there only a couple of times a summer, and it was less important than the beach.

Back in Grand Rapids, summer amusement meant Ramona Park, the great playground for most East Siders, with its rides, its old vaudeville theater, its concessions, and the miniature train that carried smaller kids around the grounds. Jerry's family lived fairly close to Ramona throughout his boyhood, but it was especially close — within easy walking distance — after they moved to East Grand Rapids before his senior year of high school.

Oddly, there is no mention of his visiting the park as a youngster, but he did have a job there in the summer before his senior year of high school, when he was saving to buy a car of his own. On week-

Ramona Park, 1929

ends and holidays, he hauled cases of Cracker Jacks and crates of pop for Alex Demar, who operated all the food and beverage concession stands. Demar years later recalled a busy July 4th when the other two high-school boys who were working for him with Jerry slipped away to take in the Marcus Girls Revue in the theater and left Jerry to stock all the concession booths by himself.

Demar had not known young Ford before that summer, except by his reputation as a high-school football star. Thus he expected a little ego, a little attitude. He was impressed to find his new employee low-key, well-spoken, respectful, and, as the July 4th incident showed, capable and more responsible than many adolescents. In later years Demar would act on that perception by becoming a loyal booster of Ford's political campaigns in the close-knit Greek community of western Michigan. The adultlike conduct that impressed him was something young Jerry repeatedly displayed, either in a work situation or a less-structured setting. Margaret Murphy, whose parents ran the store and lunchroom where the big hotel had been at Ottawa Beach, saw the Ford family every summer and remembered him — and his whole family — as easy to get along with. Kay Whinery, whose family owned a cottage, added that Jerry was like a camp counselor as a teenager.

"Jerry took the kids on hikes," she said, "He taught them how to play tennis and so on. He was wonderful with young people."

As he grew up, kids in the Union Avenue neighborhood came to look up to him as a model of behavior. His neighbor across the street, Don Nichols, who became his freshman roommate at the University of Michigan, recalled that he thought of Jerry as the ideal all-American boy: clean-cut and serious, with high standards. Don's younger brother Bill remembered Ford's kindness: "When his parents were gone he'd take me in the living room and show me how to center a football." This same kind of behavior was what won him favorable comments from teachers through his entire school career.

Part of what all these people saw was a product of Dorothy Ford's social training. All the Ford boys sat up straight, dressed neatly, and used all the correct courtesy phrases because they had been taught to do so. Young Jerry, at his mother's insistence, took ballroom dancing every Saturday at Aunt Marjory's studio after he got through swimming at the YMCA. Periodically, Marjory Ford held a full-scale dance for her pupils, which gave them a chance to display their skills; by the end of high school, Jerry was an expert, relaxed dancer. Some of his earliest correspondence shows that he carefully wrote thank-you notes — such as the one to the state park commissioner from Detroit or the one to Coach Harry Kipke at Ann Arbor — that involved social invitations and courtesies. He knew the formulas, the correct things to say on formal occasions. He wrote stilted letters to the editor of the newspaper on sports topics, and his written notes for a pregame talk to the student body are in proper grammar but sound like something from the era of Theodore Roosevelt: "I hope we shall see a good crowd of you out at our game next Saturday." But his knowledge of proper behavior impressed adults and reassured people who were ready to think of him as an unschooled athlete.

But most of the favorable impression Jerry made came from his own character: his interest in people, something he inherited no doubt from his mother, his desire to work with them, and his sensitivity to their needs. Understanding people — avoiding hurt feelings, knowing the proper response to use in handling a difficult situation — gradually emerged as his greatest talent, more visible during his adult years, when he had responsible positions, but evident on occasion even when he was a youngster, when he was more often a member of a group. It was the quality that a longtime friend from Grand Rapids, Jack Stiles, referred to in later years: "People say that Jerry doesn't have the grey matter, but I'll tell you something. It's true that he isn't a reader of books, that he's no academic, but he has a computer between his ears. He listens well and he retains it."

Group life was life, as far as Jerry was concerned; it was hard to imagine him doing anything alone. Other people were central to his concept of living, and when he did something for fun it was apt to be as part of a group of which he was already a member: as a small child, his family; at puberty, his Scout troop; in high school, his teammates; in college, his fraternity brothers. His idea of fun was to get such a group together in a situation, like the beach, where there was activity for everyone to pursue. Activity — physical or mental — was the key: passive entertainment did not appeal to him.

He went to movies or the theater if the group went, but he got little enjoyment from either the theater or the group. It was like watching another person's fantasy and experiencing no involvement. When asked in maturity to name a favorite actor, he answered, "None." For the same reason, as Stiles observed, he did not read for entertainment; reading was solitary and passive. On the other hand, he liked bridge, which he had learned from watching his parents, who played the card game regularly. Indoor and sedentary though it was, it was also competitive and interactive. In high school he had a small group of friends with whom he played bridge regularly.

Ford was slower to catch on to the one-on-one relationships that led into the dating and mating of adult life. His mother, always concerned for her son's social progress, arranged a few dates for him as he neared high school, and he was compliant as always; but he was more or less going through the motions. One time he took a girl to an event downtown, and when it was over, he put her on the streetcar to her home, taking another one in the direction of his house. He took a lot of kidding from his family about that. As for arranging dates on his own, he seemed clueless. Virginia, the girl in history with whom he used to compare grades, remembered hinting to him that he should come over to her house some time — but getting no response from him. "He was like a big Saint Bernard," she remembered. "The mind of a boy in the body of a man."

All this began to change in tenth grade, when Jerry Ford became a football star, known throughout the city by virtue of both newspapers' heavy coverage of high-school football. Girls in his own class, the South High Class of 1931, had long "worshiped him from afar." Now there began to be hints of pressure even from his teammates that he needed to have a steady girl for social functions. Players often got together for bowling or some kind of amusement, each player with a girl at his side. They thought Jerry needed to get one, too.

In his junior year he found one. She was a cute, curly-haired, and outgoing senior named Mary Hondorp, and she was also a competitive swimmer. She began going places with Jerry, and before long the girls of the junior class understood that he was "spoken for," in the words of Dorothy Gray, the attractive class valedictorian of Jerry's junior class. Mary came from a big Dutch family on the far South Side, and though her background made her an unlikely lifetime partner for Jerry, he clearly enjoyed her company. (In fact, he continued going out with her for some years after he left Grand Rapids for the University of Michigan.) Like both of the other women he was to date regularly — a model/tennis player and a dancer (his eventual wife, Betty Bloomer) — she shared his outlook on life and his fondness for sports, games, and dances.

Mary Hondorp; picture from Ford's scrapbook

As senior year approached, the tempo of social life speeded up, with class dances and club parties in addition to the get-togethers with fellow players for bowling, food, and dancing, or quick excursions to the lake. Jerry and Mary were in the thick of it, and Jerry was universally popular. Aided by his intuitive understanding of people, he stayed away from the ego clashes and emotional dramas that marked so much of his classmates' adolescence. He felt that enmities and dislikes were a waste of time. His philosophy was simple: "Everyone, I decided, had more good qualities than bad. If I understood and tried to accentuate those good qualities in others, I could get along much better."

His success can be seen in the recollections of his classmates. Allan Elliott, the starting quarterback and one of Jerry's closest friends on and off the field, put it this way: "We knew Jerry as a real live peer that we respected and admired. He was a very popular person, not only with his teammates but with other male and female students. He had his adolescent love affairs, as did we all. He dated the prettiest and most popular gals and attended all school dances as well as other social events in the city. He enjoyed playing bridge with a group of his friends. In addition to his social life, he seemed not to have neglected, as some of us might have, spiritual life . . . ." Bill Schuiling, the class president, said simply, "Nobody had a bad word for Jerry Ford."

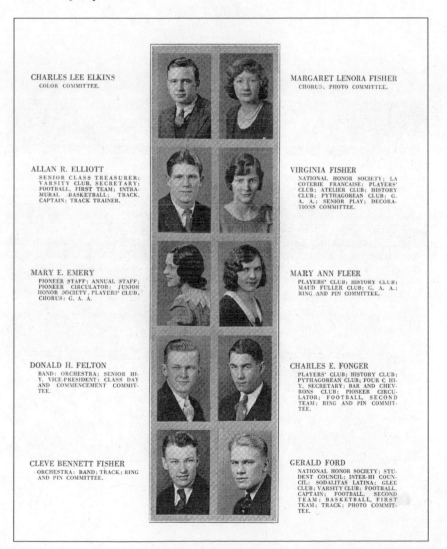

CHARLES LEE ELKINS
COLOR COMMITTEE.

MARGARET LENORA FISHER
CHORUS, PHOTO COMMITTEE.

ALLAN R. ELLIOTT
SENIOR CLASS TREASURER; VARSITY CLUB, SECRETARY; FOOTBALL, FIRST TEAM; INTRA-MURAL BASKETBALL; TRACK, CAPTAIN; TRACK TRAINER.

VIRGINIA FISHER
NATIONAL HONOR SOCIETY; LA COTERIE FRANCAISE; PLAYERS' CLUB; ATELIER CLUB; HISTORY CLUB; PYTHAGOREAN CLUB; G. A. A.; SENIOR PLAY; DECORA-TIONS COMMITTEE.

MARY E. EMERY
PIONEER STAFF; ANNUAL STAFF; PIONEER CIRCULATOR; JUNIOR HONOR SOCIETY, PLAYERS' CLUB, CHORUS; G. A. A.

MARY ANN FLEER
PLAYERS' CLUB; HISTORY CLUB; MAUD FULLER CLUB; G. A. A.; RING AND PIN COMMITTEE.

DONALD H. FELTON
BAND; ORCHESTRA; SENIOR HI-Y, VICE-PRESIDENT; CLASS DAY AND COMMENCEMENT COMMIT-TEE.

CHARLES E. FONGER
PLAYERS' CLUB; HISTORY CLUB; PYTHAGOREAN CLUB; FOUR C HI-Y, SECRETARY; BAR AND CHEV-RONS CLUB; PIONEER CIRCU-LATOR; FOOTBALL, SECOND TEAM; RING AND PIN COMMIT-TEE.

CLEVE BENNETT FISHER
ORCHESTRA; BAND; TRACK; RING AND PIN COMMITTEE.

GERALD FORD
NATIONAL HONOR SOCIETY; STU-DENT COUNCIL; INTER-HI COUN-CIL; SODALITAS LATINA; GLEE CLUB; VARSITY CLUB; FOOTBALL, CAPTAIN; FOOTBALL, SECOND TEAM; BASKETBALL, FIRST TEAM; TRACK; PHOTO COMMIT-TEE.

Allan Elliott and Jerry Ford on the same page in the 1931 *Pioneer*

Junie Ford ready
to play football

6 "Hey, Whitey, You're a Center"

A hundred fifteen-year-olds in ratty uniforms — well over half the boys in the eighth grade — milled around on the bare playground of Jefferson School, not a blade of grass on the whole dusty field. Junior Ford, with his radiant, tousled blond hair, was among them. It was a big day in the spring of 1927, the day spring football practice began, the day eighth-grade boys got their first chance to try out for the "second team" for the next fall.

So popular was football that every boy in the class with a trace of athletic ability was out on the practice field. The potential payoff was huge. If they were to make the second team that following year, and the varsity a year or two after that, thousands of adults in Grand Rapids would come out to see them play, and their performance would be the conversation of a thousand households and offices. Even if they spent most of their time on the bench, they would still be known as football players and thus popular at school.

"Why don't you go out for football?" a boy in a 1920s story was asked. "You'll never be popular till you do."

Already the king of high-school sports, football in the twenties was on its way to becoming mass entertainment for middle-class people in cities that did not have a major college. But the political consensus was still that competitive team sports were extracurricu-

87

lar and did not deserve support from the school budget. So the South High team had no field of its own; rather, it practiced on the playground of a neighboring elementary school and had barely enough uniforms to outfit its first-string players.

Head coach Cliff Gettings — tall, rangy, and fair-haired, only a few years out of college — dominated the scene, scrutinizing boys, organizing them into teams, and watching them play. As he was looking them over, he quickly sized up Junior Ford physically with his coach's eye. The latter was "long and lanky and looked [as if] he was going to be big," Gettings said. Junior was clearly cut out to be a lineman, with some indications of football intelligence — maybe worth trying at center.

"Hey, Whitey," Gettings shouted, "you're a center!" He passed Junior a football and told him to start centering. As Ford remembered it in later years, "He saw me, I had white hair, and he needed a center." Ford obediently took his place on the line and began learning how to snap a football. It was an important position: a center needed to be a strong blocker (Ford's size had caught Gettings's attention) and at the same time know how to snap the ball to start a whole repertory of different plays. In those days, a center had to snap the ball not only to the quarterback and punter, but also to a moving fullback or halfback.

Ford was at practice religiously for the rest of the spring, and by the semester's end he was sure of a place on the second team — what other schools called the "junior varsity" — in the fall. But there was more. Wherever he went outside class, he always had a football and wanted to practice.

"You never saw him without that football," recalled Joe Russo, the short, muscular Italian kid who started at fullback. "He was always after me to practice with him." A center had to polish his skills by practicing with the quarterback and running backs, and young Ford, whether he knew it or not, had understood a great truth of football: a player reached mastery by repeating his movements so often that he could execute them without thinking. Machine-like precision without conscious thought was the goal, and Ford reached it before many of his teammates did.

Coach Gettings used a double-wing formation, and Junior spent hours learning how to snap the ball to all the moving running backs, as well as to the quarterback and punter. Today's centers — in variants of the T-formation — look straight ahead and simply snap the ball to the quarterback. But in the single- or double-wing formation of the 1920s, the center was forced to view everything upside down and then had to be very quick to make a block on the opposing lineman, who had the jump on him. As Ford put it in later years, "You had to perfect different types of snaps. If the fullback was coming into the line, you had to drop the ball softly in his hands as he was moving forward. The snap for a punt had to be on the kicker's right hip. If the tailback was running left or right, you had to lead him an arm's length in the right direction."

After earning the rank of Eagle Scout during the summer of 1927 at Camp Shawondossee, Junior was visibly bigger and stronger, and he was eager to take his place on the line when practice began in September. The coach of the second team was "Pop" Churm, an easygoing history teacher who had been at South since it opened and was also an advisor for the senior class. Traveling with the varsity to out-of-town games, second teams competed against their counterparts at other high schools in games that started typically an hour or two before the Saturday afternoon main event. (Night games were still to come; some Lansing schools would be the first in Michigan, in 1930, to experiment with artificially lighted football games at night.) Few spectators other than die-hard football fans took in the second-team games, but the coaches kept a close eye on their performance, judging their potential for a place on next year's varsity. They liked what they saw in Ford — "Junie" to his teammates by this time — who was not only a competent center but a kind of informal team leader. He kept the players motivated and united and was a natural competitor with a good grasp of the game. He would never be a running back (though Churm experimented with him in the backfield) because he lacked speed, but he was an aggressive blocker.

Aggressiveness, in fact, was also his major problem: he began to develop a reputation as a hotheaded player not always in control of himself. Early in his football career, probably in ninth grade, Ford's team happened to play in a game officiated by Paul Goebel, a friend of Jerry Sr. and owner of a downtown sporting-goods store who had himself been a starting player at the University of Michigan. As Goebel recalled, the younger Ford had a problem with an opponent during that game, and both players were getting testy. When the other player did something Ford didn't like during a pileup, Ford got to his feet and gave him "a good, hard belt in the chops."

"You're out of this game," Goebel shouted at him, and Junie walked off the field without argument. This behavior was just a sample. By the next year, when he was on the varsity, Ford had a reputation among the referees and was charged fairly regularly with fouls he hadn't committed.

What was happening, of course, was the Leslie King flashes of fury showing themselves, and Coach Gettings had to explain to Junie that an established tactic in competitive sports was to throw one's opponent off balance by getting him mad. To be a good player he would have to learn to give up the satisfaction of belting an annoying opponent for the greater satisfaction of helping his team win the official victory over the opponents. Gradually Junie learned to do that. All the dramatic explosions of temper were over by his senior year; the anger was still there, but it was under control.

Junie spent the better part of the summer of 1928 on the staff at Shawondossee, knowing that he had a place on the varsity for the next fall, as the backup center to Orris Burghdorf. But shortly before the season started, Burghdorf was injured, and Junie Ford, with his good record from the junior varsity, seemed the next best bet. Junie played the first few games of the season, and by the time Burghdorf had recovered, the sophomore had established himself. Junie started the rest of the season.

Presented With City Championship Football Trophy

Above is the South high school city championship football team of 1928, with a picture of the city championship trophy, presented last night by the Grand Rapids Elks lodge at the annual father and sons' banquet. Of the first squad of 20 pictured above, Coach Cliff Gettings will have 11 back next fall and South is already looking forward to another successful year.

Those in the picture are, left to right: First row—Walter Graves, Orris Bergdorf, Marvin Barclay, Elton Holland (captain), Lester Nelson, Richard Zylstra, Charles Rogers.

Second Row—Stanley Keeler, Joe Russo (1929 captain-elect), Allen Elliott, Forest Johnson. Lyle Breen, Ules Ketchum, Gerald Ford.

Back Row—Coach Cliff Gettings, Roy Dolson (manager), Don Hubbard, Louis Fuller, Austin Snyder, Fred Harker, Arthur Brown, Harold Ackershook.

Now that he was on the varsity team, the crowds were larger and the games were written up in the city newspapers. The band, with its giant drum and the male cheerleaders (or "yell leaders") added color to the games, though serious players like Ford, their minds focused on winning, simply blotted them out. Despite the crowds, however, football still lacked material support from the schools and the community. Like most Grand Rapids high-school teams, the Trojans of South played their games at Island Park, a centrally located "pebble-filled, rough, muddy" field in which the last three yards at one end went uphill. Other communities where South played had similar

1928 South High football team; Ford in second row, at right

fields: at a game during wet weather against Holland High, for example, there were six inches of water on the last ten yards at one end, and the referee had to hold the ball in place so that it wouldn't float away. The red-and-blue South High uniforms were a similar problem: there were never enough to go around, and some were in really bad condition. At the beginning of the 1929 season their appearance became so scandalous that the problem came before the school board.

By today's standards, the game of the 1920s was primitive. It was still the era of the rounder ball; not until 1934 was the ball's diameter slimmed down to its present size. There were no hash marks on the field, so every down began where the previous play had ended, even if it was only a yard from the sidelines. Scoreboards, where they existed, were manual, not electric, and only the scorekeeper knew how much time was left in a period. The equipment itself was much simpler: leather helmets ("you could sure feel it if you got rapped pretty hard on the head," said one South player), no face masks (Ford's teammate Russ Koepnick would become one of innumerable high-school boys who broke their noses playing football), no tape, and little protective gear of any kind beyond the basic hip and shoulder pads.

The school year began on September 4, and the first game, with Davis Technical School, was scheduled for the fifteenth. Davis was one of South's rivals for the city championship, though South seemed to have little prospect of winning. Gettings's record in his short career at South had been unimpressive. He was just out of college and still feeling his way; his 1927 varsity had won just three games and lost six. But in the 1928 season the fortunes of the "Red and Blue" began to change. When they played Davis, it looked at first like the start of another mediocre season. Neither team had its game together: the first half was marked by "sloppy football" and pathetic fumbles. In the third quarter, Ford made a bad snap from center, the halfback dropped the ball, and Davis recovered the fumble and scored. But in the fourth quarter, just in time, the South team found its passing game, scored two touchdowns, and won 12-7. Likewise, the second game, against Creston, another city rival, was a scoreless tie for three quarters and most of the fourth; but then the South quarterback, thanks to a good snap from Ford, faked a punt and threw a long forward pass with only three minutes to go. South scored the only touchdown of the game and seemed to have a chance at the city championship.

The same pattern recurred in two later games that season: a scoreless tie in the first half in which the teams seemed evenly matched, followed by a second half in which South won by a single touchdown. As the list of victories piled up, sports reporters began taking Gettings's team more seriously and extolling the ball carriers in the flowery language of the day. Lester Nelson, the light-skinned African-American track star who played halfback, became "Lightning Les," and Joe Russo, the fullback, was likened to an "infuriated ox." The linemen, as usual, received less attention, but Ford was mentioned at least once by name. Crowds began turning out at Island Park to follow their progress toward the city championship.

Progress, however, was not uninterrupted. On October 13 the Red and Blue were defeated by the team from Muskegon, a gritty industrial town that took its football very seriously. Even so, the score was only 19-12, and South's passing game continued to be impressive. By the middle of November, with two weeks to go in the season, South had a 7-1 record, and Junie Ford was experiencing the rush of being part of a star football team, accompanied by the buzz in the school corridors and the friendly comments downtown. Dorothy Ford began keeping a scrapbook to record her son's exploits.

The last two games were a bit of a letdown. Both were matches against traditional rivals. Holland, the little town on Lake Michigan, was generally an easy opponent for South, but not this year. The game was played at Holland in a pouring rain that eventually drove away all the spectators except a few die-hards from Grand Rapids and completely neutralized Gettings's passing attack. Covered in mud that obscured their uniforms and numbers, the teams struggled back and forth through great ponds of standing water on the field, raising fears among the spectators that someone would drown before the game was over. The play was "indifferent," according to sports reporters, and the outcome was a 6-6 tie.

There was dry weather for the final game at Island Park against South's traditional crosstown rival, Union, the working-class high school on the West Side whose stars had names like Bozo Brzowski and Eddie Piechocki. South had already won the city championship by defeating all its other city rivals, but a Thanksgiving victory over Union would be especially sweet, following three consecutive losses in preceding seasons. City football fans in general were anticipating a major clash, a "spectacular encounter" as the *Grand Rapids Herald* put it. More than 10,000 jammed Island Park and watched from neighboring rooftops and boxcars. But, except to Union fans, the game was a disappointment. The West Siders dominated the field all afternoon, even into the dusk that closed the game. None of Gettings's plays seemed to work as they were supposed to. The South team could not seem to get it together, and they lost by a score of 12-0.

The bitterest disappointment to Junie was that he had to watch most of the game from the bench. In the first quarter an official sent him off the field for kneeing a Union player in the ribs, and Burghdorf played the rest of the game. Ford was adamant, even years later, that it was a bad call, that he hadn't done anything unsportsmanlike. But he was keenly embarrassed at being on the sidelines while his teammates were hard-pressed in the center of the field. His reputation for roughness had hurt not only him but the team as a whole.

Two days later, however, there was an unexpected consolation, when the *Herald* announced its selections for the All-City team. Several of the city teams had good centers, with Union's Tony Dauksza probably the outstanding one. But Dauksza had been out much of the season, and so had Bert Koning of Central. Weighing all the factors, Heinie Martin of the *Herald* judged Ford the year's best center, for "his hard, earnest, and aggressive work all season." The selection meant a photo on the front page of the Sunday sports section, duly clipped and pasted into his scrapbook by Dorothy, another on a special page in the *South High Pioneer* that June, and a first taste of wider public recognition.

For the rest of his sophomore year, Ford slipped into the unexpected role of school football hero. Bill Skougis offered him a lunchtime job at his hamburger shack across the street, both as his way of supporting the team and because a football star behind the counter was good for sales. Junie also became a member of the track team — along with almost all his teammates from varsity football — because Gettings insisted that his players stay in shape throughout the year. Gettings assigned Junie to the strength events, discus and shot put, not the speed events. Ford would actually become pretty good at shot put over the next three years, and he would help South win several meets.

Increasingly, Junie hung around with his football and track teammates on and off the field, becoming a real "jock," though that word was not yet in use in the 1920s and '30s. Allan Elliott, the quarterback, was one of his close friends; but an even closer buddy was Arthur Brown, who, despite his surname, was a hulking Italian who lined up next to Junie on the offensive line. Brown, whose father owned a drugstore where team members often gathered, "was not the best academic student, but he was a hell of a football player," Ford recalled years later. "I was in a class with him our senior year. . . . It looked like he might fail; and if he failed he couldn't play football. So I really kicked his ass and made him work, and he passed." Brown's version was that they shared a desk, and the combination of Junie's left-handedness and his right-handed orientation made it possible for him to get direct help from glances at Junie's paper as supplements to the latter's encouragement. He believed that Ford was unaware of that source of help.

As a group, the South High varsity footballers thought of themselves as dead-end kids, working-class guys to whom values and academics were not particularly important, and their outlook became a part of Ford's social life for the rest of his high-school years. Some of the stories about him and his friends have a kind of dumb-jock quality: for example, the one about the girl who shared a tenth-grade class with some of them, including Junie, and found them blocking the aisle with their legs so that she couldn't get back to her seat. Then there was the time Junie and Brown decided, just for fun, to ride the school elevator, which was reserved for faculty, only to come face to face with a district administrator. Or the time some team members, riding around in their car during junior year, spotted Junie's car parked in front of Mary Hondorp's house, pushed it around the corner, and waited to enjoy his reaction when he came out and found it missing. His consternation, followed by his rage when he discovered the trick, was everything they had hoped for.

The summer of 1929, before his junior year at South High, was a hybrid between Junie's old life as a Boy Scout and his new one as a football player. He continued working at Bill's, but he also took time to be on the staff at Shawondossee to teach swimming to younger Scouts. In August he suddenly found himself on Mackinac Island, again representing the Grand Rapids area council of the Boy Scouts of America. But his thoughts were already focused on the coming season. His reputation in Scouting was now a sure thing. But he still had one reputation to make, in South High football, and he plunged into practice the first week of September.

Gettings was a real taskmaster, and he would work his players long and hard. Sometimes they wouldn't get home until eight o'clock at night. Part of the reason for his strictness was his sense that the guys on the team — most of them — were foul-mouthed street kids who needed discipline in their lives before they could concentrate on the game. He enforced a rule against four-letter words at practice: one offense meant one extra lap around the track, two offenses meant two, and so on. With the endless practice of fundamentals and the conditioning drills, Gettings interspersed earnest but clean talks designed to motivate the players, to stir them up into a fighting mood. During one session he noticed a couple of players laughing and whispering. Annoyed, he ended the practice and dismissed the whole team, and they filed off the field. But ten or fifteen minutes later they came back, led by Junie Ford as their spokesman. He apologized for their lack of attention and asked for practice to resume. That was the kind of boy leader he was, Gettings recalled in later years.

"Having Jerry on that team was like having another coach on the field." The team recognized it as well. More and more, they counted on him to hold them together. When, in the middle of the season, Joe Russo had to quit because he had turned twenty and was too old for high-school sports, it was understood that Junie would be captain in 1930, even though by that time he was injured and playing only part of the time.

High-school footballers had to develop a fatalistic attitude about injuries. With the minimal protective gear they wore, it could happen — and probably would. So it was unsurprising, but still a big blow to the team, when Junie suffered a knee injury three weeks into the season. It did not happen in a pileup during a game, but at a practice, and it was the classic "trick knee": a tiny floating pad of cartilage in the joint that could lock his right knee painfully motionless at times and make it feel weak and unstable at others. Ford was stoical about it: he wanted to play, but sometimes the injury got the better of him, and Pete Dood, the backup center, would take his place. Massage was the standard treatment of the time. "Bosh" Bosscher, Junie's comrade from the YMCA swimming team, who also served as student trainer for the football team, remembered rubbing Ford's knee for the better part of an hour before every game; unfortunately, it had little lasting effect. As the season went on, Gettings compromised: he left Ford at home for road games and used Dood. To Jerry, this situation had to be more painful than the knee itself: missing four games in a ten-game season would destroy his chance to repeat as an all-city player. And if the injury persisted, it could be the end of his football career.

It was at this point that Danny Rose appeared in Jerry's life. The consequences were momentous.

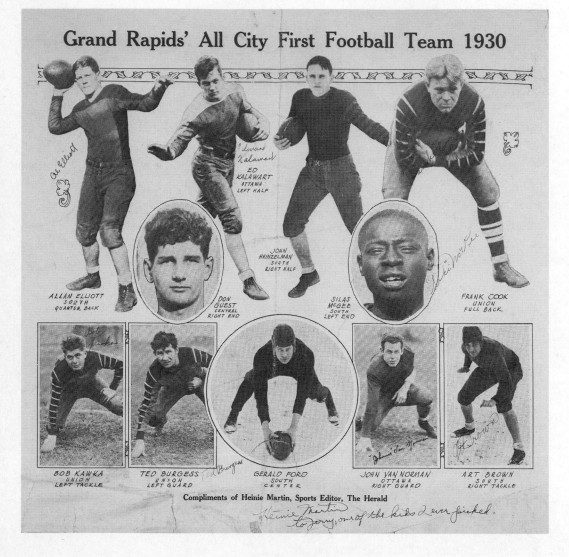

Grand Rapids' All City First Football Team 1930

ALLAN ELLIOTT
SOUTH
QUARTER BACK

ED KALAWART
OTTAWA
LEFT HALF

DON GUEST
CENTRAL
RIGHT END

JOHN HEINZELMAN
SOUTH
RIGHT HALF

SILAS McGEE
SOUTH
LEFT END

FRANK COOK
UNION
FULL BACK

BOB KAWKA
UNION
LEFT TACKLE

TED BURGESS
UNION
LEFT GUARD

GERALD FORD
SOUTH
CENTER

JOHN VAN NORMAN
OTTAWA
RIGHT GUARD

ART BROWN
SOUTH
RIGHT TACKLE

Compliments of Heinie Martin, Sports Editor, The Herald

The *Grand Rapids Press* all-city football team of 1930

7 The Athlete

Treatment for a floating meniscus, today a routine outpatient surgery, was in the late 1920s generally a plaster cast and bed rest for a week or two (which some worried could lead to atrophy) — or massages. Surgery was risky because of the possibility of infection. Massage brought only temporary relief. As the South High team plodded its way to a lackluster 5-5 season, Junie and his dad, whose new manufacturing company was making its debut at just that time, met with Coach Gettings to consider the options, none of which seemed to be an ideal choice.

It was a stroke of good fortune that, precisely at that moment, a star of Michigan sports entered Junie's life — the diminutive but aggressive Danny Rose. Rose was a startlingly bright kid from an Italian immigrant family in tiny Rogers City, Michigan, who had managed to find the money to attend the University of Michigan, where he had embarked on a pre-med academic program. But when the dean of the Medical School told him he had to give up basketball to succeed as a pre-med student, he switched his major to physical education and became the star of Michigan's basketball team. He achieved that status, despite being only 5 feet 8 inches tall, through sheer intelligence and hustle. After graduating from Michigan in 1929, he took his first job teaching four classes of anatomy and

FIRST TEAM BASKETBALL

Top Row—Mr. Rose, Walter Johnson, Peter Dood, Henry Jipping, Hugh Holt, Silas McGee, Mr. Wickett.
First Row—Edward Preston, Martin Geyer, Leon Joslin, Robert Eckardt, Gerald Ford, Louis Cooley, John Heinzelman.

South High's basketball team, 1930-31

GETTINGS   ROSE   CHURM   WICKETT

The South High coaches, 1931

physiology at South High School, plus coaching the basketball team and backing up the football program.

Young Mr. Rose both fascinated and intimidated his classroom students at South High with his knowledge and his rigorous teaching. But he also managed to be concerned about them as people. His intensity and high standards — along with his problem-solving savvy — quickly earned him a good reputation in the halls and ball fields of the school. At the end of the football season, with Junie Ford's knee problem still unresolved, Danny joined the discussions about what to do next. His experience in Ann Arbor, where the football program had strong financial support, was more up-to-date than that of anyone else at South High at the time. Orthopedic surgery, he told them, had improved radically since World War I; infection, for example, was no longer a hazard. He had seen cases like Junie's successfully treated at University Hospital in Ann Arbor.

As the Ford family's relationship with Coach Rose grew, they recognized a young man with "the same basic concepts as to citizenship and character" that they held, in the words of the future president. Rose, always polite and professional, offered to drive Jerry to the University himself, to introduce him to his friends on the athletic staff and in the hospital, and to get his knee assessed. Mr. and Mrs. Ford were impressed and grateful.

It may have been Junie's first visit to Ann Arbor. He saw the Gothic campus quadrangle, the gigantic Michigan Stadium, and the massive hospital with a new wing under construction. Rose introduced him to the trainer, Charles Hoyt, the dynamic coach, Harry Kipke, and perhaps even the famous athletic director, Fielding Yost. Carl Badgley, who was one of the country's best orthopedic surgeons — and an early specialist in what would later be called "sports medicine" — examined his knee.

At some point during a school break early in 1930, Dr. Badgley operated successfully on Junie's knee. No athletic program picked up the fee for the surgery, but Jerry Sr., knowing how much football meant to his son, willingly put up the money. For the younger Ford,

Michigan Stadium in the 1920s, already a vast "temple of sport" (from an etching by Wilfred Byron Shaw, 1881-1959)

the operation and the first contact with college athletics were a turning point. The operation put him back on the field and also introduced him to a higher, more serious level of athletic achievement that he tried to adopt over the rest of his time in high school.

The Ford family's move to East Grand Rapids prior to his senior year presented two practical problems for Junie. The little suburb had its own high school, only a block from the Fords' Lake Drive house, and under ordinary circumstances he would be expected to enroll and play football with the team there. But as captain of the next fall's squad at South, he felt special obligations. Through Gettings he got permission from the city school district to finish his

high school career at South; then he called Reed Waterman, the athletic director at East Grand Rapids, in person to explain his decision and express his regret at not being able to play for East. Waterman thought that he handled the call very well.

2163 Lake Drive, East Grand Rapids, the Ford family home, 1930-32

The other problem was distance. The new house was three miles away from South High, two miles farther from the school than the old house was. Junie, like many a sixteen-year-old, was getting tired of walking, so he considered walking three miles to school out of the question. And the route to school by streetcar was long and awkward. He needed a car. Some of his friends on the team drove their own cars, and occasionally he drove his father's car. Anyone over fourteen could get a license in the 1920s, and nothing like formal driver training existed. Youngsters simply began driving when they could afford to. The following summer Junie worked three jobs: one for Alex Demar at Ramona Park; filling cans of paint for his father; and flipping hamburgers at Bill's. By summer's end, the seventy-five bucks he had saved bought a battered but treasured 1924 Ford coupe.

The knee operation had had no visible effect on Jerry's school-work during his junior year. He continued to get A's in history, B's and C's in everything else, and scraped along with a constant C in Latin, which he loathed. By track season, he was back at shot put, reconnecting with football teammates like Leon Joslin, who threw discus, and Siki (pronounced "Psyche") McGee, who ran the hundred-yard dash and played end in football. McGee was the only African-American on the varsity, a speedy runner who cultivated the persona of a clown, deliberately parodying black entertainers of the day with funny walks in the halls and snappy dances at parties. Bob Eckhardt, another runner, did not play football, only basketball and track. But he had a car, and he often drove Junie home from track practice.

Ford Paint and Varnish Company had a seasonal business: the local painters who were its customers did the great majority of their work in warm weather. As June approached, extra employees were needed. Junie was one, and he also got a job for his friend Allan Elliott. They filled paint cans, cleaned vats, pasted labels, and toned their muscles by doing the heavy work of shifting 150-pound drums of paint around the factory floor. The few other workers in the factory agreed that Junie got no breaks from being the owner's son. Junie and Allen talked football, and they considered their plans for the fall.

The last season's disappointments still rankled, including the failure to win the city championship; but the team had high hopes for 1930. With the number of lettermen returning to the roster, they expected to have a first-rate team. Then there was also a matter of payback to take care of. In the first game of 1929, they had unexpectedly lost 10-6 to Ottawa Hills, the brand-new East Side school. The first game on their 1930 schedule was against Ottawa, and they did not intend to lose again.

Junie came up with the idea of a conditioning camp, with some exercises, the way big-time college teams did it. It could be held at the cabin on the Pere Marquette that the Fords co-owned, the week

At "training camp." Clockwise from left: Art Brown, Ford, Dick "Swede" Zylstra, Leon Joslin

before school began. He knew the playbook, and they could work through it. Without consulting Gettings, he recruited fifteen team members. Junie's father agreed to chaperone. The first night, two groups got to scuffling around and knocked a hole in the plaster-board wall, which upset Junie — until his father said it was okay. When they got to work, they played hard, with Ottawa in mind, and, as Gettings said later, "when they came out of there, brother, they were *mean*."

The Ottawa Hills game would be fought out on South's new foot-ball field, next to the school — built the previous year and paid for with a bond issue by the school's alumni — and anticipation was high. South fans were not let down, as Elliott scored all three touchdowns in a convincing 18-6 win. Ford's north-woods preseason camp was seen as key to the victory, at least by someone at Ottawa Hills, and the school filed a protest with the state high school athletic association, citing a violation of the regulation against early practice. Called to Lansing to explain, Gettings convinced the association that it was a totally volunteer effort by dedicated players, and the victory stayed on the record.

In the training-camp episode, Junie Ford effectively played the role of assistant coach, and he did so repeatedly throughout the season. He knew the playbook by heart, and his memory for details of the actual plays in a game was phenomenal, according to Edward Preston, a teammate who recalled Junie's postgame sessions. Principal Krause actually encouraged Ford, rather than Gettings, to take responsibility for the team. At the beginning of the season Gettings, thinking Ford had the head of a running back, moved him off the line — but not for long. "I wasn't very agile," Ford remembered.

Backfield or line, it didn't matter — he had a great time. He drove his car to school and then used it to transport his teammates to practice at Garfield Park, with several hanging on the running boards. He and Art Brown, or his fullback, "Swede" Zylstra, used it for double-dating — that is, when it was running. It was often in the auto mechanics class at South, being used as an instructional subject for shop students. That coupe was, as Bill Schuiling, the class president, remembered, "not much of a car," but it meant the world to the future world leader.

As the Trojans kept logging victories, it became clear that the 1930 team was very bold — maybe unstoppable. Besides Elliott, a fine quarterback, and McGee, a speedy end, Junie Ford was being applauded as fearless. In those years before offensive and defensive specialization — and limited substitution — he played both offense and defense. On defense he played linebacker, or what they called "roving center" at that time.

"One of the main things about Jerry," Art Brown said, "was that he could never find enough guys to throw a block at. He'd knock down his assigned man and then jump up and look for somebody else." And as tackler on defense, he was just as good.

"He was all over the field making tackles," Coach Gettings said. "He seemed to be able to run faster when he was chasing somebody than he could if they were chasing him." Jim Trimpe, the backup halfback, put it this way: "When I was on defense, it was always great to see Ford up ahead as linebacker. By the time I got up to the play, he usually had the ball carrier flattened." Gettings called him "one of the toughest players I ever saw."

By the early weeks of November, Gettings's (or Ford's) team had won eight successive games, the last three by identical scores of 13-0. Two games remained on the schedule: Holland High, always a thorn in South's side, and their rival from the West Side, Union High, also unbeaten, on the strength of its star running back, Frank Cook. The Holland game was, as usual, a fierce defensive battle. In the first quarter, a Ford block opened a hole wide enough for Elliott to sneak through and score. And an interception by Ford in the end zone, late in the game, saved the 7-0 victory for South.

The South-Union game, played on November 27, with two unbeaten teams fighting it out on a new field, was for years a classic piece of Grand Rapids athletic folklore. Not only was the city championship at stake, but also the state championship. A crowd estimated at 12,000 paid one dollar apiece, an unheard-of price for a high-school game, especially during the economic hard times of 1930. It was the coldest Thanksgiving weekend in recent memory, with temperatures in the teens and six inches of snow on the field — so that the lines had to be marked with bleach — and more snow falling. Numb-fingered players could not hold onto the frozen ball. Gettings had the Trojans change shoes three times, trying to get them traction on the slippery surface. Though running was next to impossible, the game was played out to its full length. The combatants fell and slid to a scoreless tie, which meant that they shared the city championship; but it also meant that neither team won the

Thanksgiving 1930 game program, with Dorothy Ford's handwritten comment

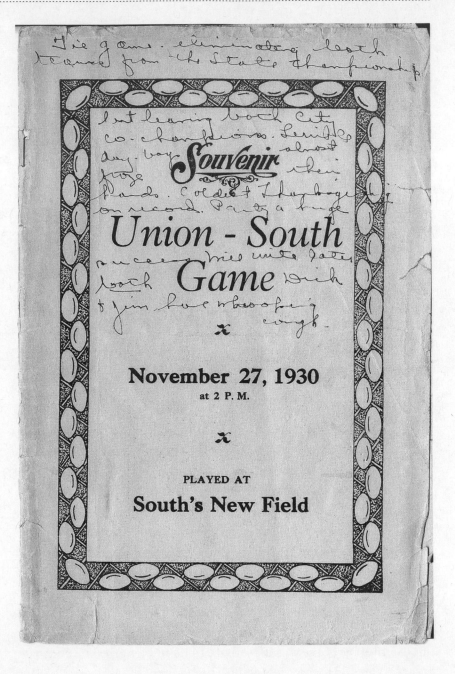

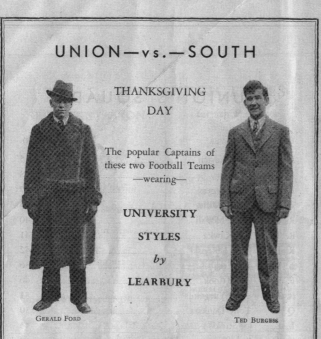
**An ad from the
Thanksgiving
1930 program**

state championship. Players and spectators left frustrated and exhausted.

The denouement came two months later, when it was revealed that Union's Frank Cook had accepted money in the fall from a major-league baseball team that he expected to sign with after graduation. This came out after a round of banquets and ceremonies at which the two teams, with great politeness, had shared city championship honors. Cook lost his amateur standing, and Union had to forfeit all its victories of the preceding season. South was, belatedly, the city and the state champion.

The whole controversy attracted statewide attention to South High and to Ford as an athlete, especially when he was named center on the all-state high school team. Various colleges expressed interest in him, through either coaches or alumni. Even before the final game of his high-school season, Junie had been approached twice by the athletic director of Michigan State University, Ralph Young. And Fred Stiles, a Harvard alumnus who lived in Grand Rapids, impressed by the young man's combination of football prowess and good grades, offered to pay his way there if he could gain admission. The offer was worth exploring, because the Depression, which had seemed to spare the paint industry during the summer, had hit Ford Paint and Varnish hard in the fall, and there was no family support to pay Jerry's way. But the plan had to be dropped when Jerry could not pass the entrance exam. The same thing happened with Northwestern University.

But the University of Michigan, with the support of Coach Danny Rose as well as Principal Krause, had the inside track. Admission was no problem at that state university: the top 15 percent of students at every high school in the state were automatically granted admission if they chose. That definitely included Junie. In the late spring, Michigan's football coach, Harry Kipke, a legendary figure in the state, drove to Grand Rapids to meet with high-school prospects, and Krause set up a meeting for him with the Fords to discuss practical arrangements. Tuition was fifty dollars a semester, and there were no athletic scholarships as such, Kipke told them. Jerry Sr. suggested that the athletic department pay him, in the form of a paint contract, in return for his son's attendance.

At that point Principal Krause, a Masonic brother of Jerry Sr., reminded him that South High had a bookstore that usually ran a small profit. He said that he was going to declare the first annual South High athletic scholarship in favor of Gerald Ford Jr., and that scholarship would contribute a hundred dollars to pay his college tuition. The hundred or so dollars that Junie could save over the summer from his salary at the paint company would go for rent and books. Kipke promised that he could get Junie good jobs working on campus as a freshman, to put spending money in his pocket. These small sources, carefully put together, would make the difference between going to college and job-hunting in the increasingly shaky business world. Thousands of American families were making similar calculations in early 1931, as the reality of the Depression bit harder into middle-class life.

Meanwhile, Jerry decided to repay his debt to Coach Rose in an improbable way: he signed up for the basketball team. He was not fast or agile, and not a terribly good shooter, but Rose's winning team from the previous season, which had lost several graduating seniors, desperately needed replacements. His technical know-how and motivational skills could transform a bulky young man into an asset for the team. And to a surprising degree, it worked.

"Dan carefully brought me along in my senior year," Ford wrote in later years, "as a member of the varsity by utilizing my defensive skills and compensating for my offensive deficiencies. He would kid me about my lack of production on field goals but praise me for holding down the scoring of the other team's best shooter." Jerry spent hours in the gym practicing field goals, which increased his shooting accuracy a bit. But he was a regular terror on defense: he was all over the opposing players — to such a degree that he often fouled out. But whether on offense or defense, he threw all his energy into the game. Fellow students recalled him charging, red-faced, as he brought the ball down the court. His recollection of the basketball experience, in maturity, was high praise for Rose: "Dan was a perfectionist. He expected every player to compete up to the maximum of his ability. . . . His relationship with his players was very serious and demanding on the one hand but relaxed and personal on the other."

Coaching began to look to Ford like a vocation that could do great personal and social good while simultaneously satisfying his desire to win. It is not perfectly clear whether Ford wanted to play basketball for the sake of the game or for the opportunity to be on a team, to observe Rose again and see how he orchestrated his forces. Had some events in the next years of his life gone differently, Ford could have been, rather than President of the United States, a high school or college coach, and no doubt a much admired one.

Ford's car barely survived football season. The first really cold night in December, with snow on the ground and nighttime temperatures below zero, he pulled into the driveway after basketball practice. Steam was coming from under the hood, so he opened it to take a look. The engine block was so hot that it was glowing a dull red. At that moment he remembered that he had put no antifreeze in the radiator. He had seen other car owners drape blankets over their hoods on really cold nights, so he decided that what this car needed for protection was a blanket over the engine itself. He covered it with an old blanket from the garage and went in to dinner. Half an hour later, his brother Tom looked out the window and saw Junie's car on fire. The family heard sirens — neighbors had already called the fire department — but by the time help arrived, it was too late. The car burned to a shell in the driveway. And, to make matters worse, Junie had to admit to his father that he had neglected his advice to take out insurance. For the rest of the year he rode the streetcar to school in the morning: all the way downtown on the Wealthy Street line, then another mile south on the Division Avenue line. At least he could usually get a ride home from practice with Bob Eckhardt.

The burning Model-T was not the only automobile that Junie was hard on during his senior year of high school. It was also in his senior year that the Ford family bought a six-passenger Chandler sedan. In the spring, when the track team had a meet in Grand Haven, thirty-five miles away, and the team had no money for traveling expenses, the track coach suggested that those who could borrow their parents' cars do so, and the rest of the team members could carpool with those individuals. Junie's stepfather agreed to allow him to drive the Chandler to the meet. The team won the track meet, but as they were leaving the parking area to return to Grand Rapids, Junie backed into a tree. The impact broke the clamp that attached the spare tire to the back of the car. Six members of the track team were crowded into the car, so the spare tire could not go there. "No problem," Ford thought. "I'll just tie the tire onto the back of the car." Not until he arrived home did he realize that the heat from the exhaust pipe had burned a hole through the spare tire. His stepfather let him have it. In the end, though insurance paid for the repair of the car, Junie had to pay for the ruined tire.

Junie spent the last months of his high-school athletic career with friends on the track team, traveling to meets as far away as Lansing and Detroit. At the same time, he and Allan Elliott competed with the YMCA swimming team at a tristate (Michigan, Ohio, and Indiana) event in Fort Wayne, Indiana. One of the fringe benefits of competitive sports, Jerry realized, was that they led to new experiences and new places. Athletics at the college level, Kipke and Rose reminded him, would open doors into a new world, not only satisfying the competitive urge and fostering team spirit, but offering its best players honors and opportunities, even money and a new style of living. The social and monetary rewards of sports would loom almost as large as the thrill of the games themselves. Indeed, Jerry realized, he could already testify to the power of athletics from his own experience.

"Many people helped," he said years later, "but football was my ticket to Michigan."

Ford for Class President on the "Progressive" ticket

VOTE
PROGRESSIVELY

FORD **PRES.**

**FOR
Student
Government**

FACULTY
ADVISERS

GETTINGS, OSSEWARDE

D. GRAY - VICE PRES.

B. POPE   -   SECRETARY

A. ELLIOT - TREASURER

STUDENT ADVISORS

**MEDENDORP, TODISH,
DOSKER**

8 Leadership, Law, and the Depression

Young Jerry Ford kept his eye on the ball — in football and in his career plans. Football was to be his ticket to the University of Michigan, but his purpose in going there remained the study of law. His steadfast commitment made him stand out. "Not many of us harbored a thought of entering college," said Allan Elliott. "Consequently, most of us selected courses of study that would get us through high school. Not Jerry. He knew what he wanted to do and what he needed to do to reach his goal: the University of Michigan and a law degree."

In his senior year, in pursuit of his goal, Ford took a course in public speaking and received a B; it appears on his transcript next to B's in typing and science, A's in physical training and American history, and his usual C in Latin. The grade in public speaking would suggest that his competence in speaking was at least average, if not above. But as most of his fellow students in the class of 1931 knew, the actual situation was different: Jerry Ford had real trouble speaking in public. As captain of the football team, he was supposed to deliver a message of encouragement at the Friday morning pep rallies, and the scrapbook his mother kept contains a typed copy of his notes for one such speech. But sometimes he couldn't get the words out.

"We wonder why the best football players make the worst

speeches on Friday mornings," the student newspaper editorialized. "Is it because their ability to make touchdowns is inversely proportional to their ability to make coherent fifteen-second speeches?" Another week's issue referred ironically to "football assemblies at which we hear the gridiron heroes display their oratorical abilities." Ford may not have been — in fact, almost surely was not — the only team member who lacked a smooth delivery, but there were other stories that singled him out. At one football banquet where he was supposed to have given a speech, he got up, gulped, stood there, and sat back down. One classmate described him this way: "His words came with a rush, they — well, 'breathless' is the nearest word. But they would not come at banquets and receptions."

Some of the time he spoke adequately; he must have done something to earn that B in public speaking. As with most people, his fluency varied with the topic under discussion. Serious, bookish James McNitt, the editor of the student literary magazine, was in the public speaking class with Ford. One day he delivered a criticism of so-called "amateur" tennis players like Bill Tilden who took money under the table, and in so doing found himself on the receiving end of a counterblast by the football captain, who either was upset by the implication that money was a widespread problem in athletics or interpreted McNitt's speech as an attack on sports in general. The latter was not quite sure which one it was. But this may have been one of those occasions when Ford's words "came with a rush."

Possibly Jerry joined the debating club in connection with his public speaking course. In later years he claimed to have been a high-school debater; but the only other story connecting him with debating in high school comes from his sophomore year, when he tried out for the team and was told by the coach, Joanna Allaben, that he might as well give up the idea. He was never on South's interscholastic debate team, which was headed by Dorothy Gray, one of the most talented students in the class of 1931, and won many state awards. In any case, what this problem meant for his career was that he was not cut out to be a courtroom lawyer. But that was not the role he saw for himself in the future anyway. He wanted to be a counselor and harmonizer, using his legal knowledge to bring about settlements out of court.

Nor did his lack of eloquence affect the respect that his classmates and teachers held for him. They looked to him not for verbal inspiration but for character, energy, and instinctive sympathy. Moreover, he had the image of a leader. Time after time in that senior year, when students were needed to represent South at a citywide event, the administration chose Jerry and Dorothy Gray. They made a marvelous pair: she was attractive and brainy, and Jerry's combination of football stardom, good looks, and good grades called to mind Gene Tunney, the educated heavyweight champion, one of the most popular figures of the 1920s.

In the fall of his senior year, when elections were held for class officers, Jerry offered himself for president on the "Progressive" ticket, with Dorothy Gray as vice president. It was the first time he had sought student office, and with the dream ticket of him and Dorothy, it should have been a walkaway. Instead, the four-week campaign turned into a wild ride that became a part of class folklore. Two other candidates unexpectedly entered the contest: Bill Schuiling, an older boy from a strict Dutch Reformed family in the country, who always wore a suit to school, running as a "Republican"; and Leo Van Tassel, student manager of the football team, on the "Universal" ticket. Seniors got heavily involved in the contest, and at a student assembly, Ford's campaign manager made some controversial remarks. Interest in the balloting, on a real voting machine that was borrowed from the Grand Rapids Board of Elections, was intense. In the end, Schuiling trounced both his rivals, with 112 votes, to 39 for Ford and 29 for Van Tassel.

That result was very surprising. Schuiling declared that, by running on the Republican label, he had garnered automatic support, since Grand Rapids was a GOP stronghold, and teenagers — like their parents — were conditioned to vote Republican. Ford, looking back on it, blamed Van Tassel's entering the race for his second-place finish. But that was not a cogent explanation, because even if his totals and Van Tassel's would have been combined, the total would still not have been a majority. What was probably the likeliest story came out several months later: Coach Gettings and the other coaches, anxious that Junie's attention might be distracted from the football field to something as frivolous as student government, had passed the word for students to vote against him if they wanted a championship football team, and they may have put Van Tassel up to entering the race as well. Whatever the cause of his loss might have been, that class election was not a fair measure of Ford's popularity.

A better test, which Jerry won, came in the spring of his senior year, when the Majestic, one of the big "movie palaces" on lower Monroe Avenue, held a competition for the "most popular high school student in the city." It was a publicity gimmick, meant to improve business for movie theaters throughout the country; even so, students became heavily involved in it from the time it was announced in late February 1931. Probably forty thousand votes were cast before balloting closed on March 31. The theater released standings every week to keep up interest. Junie, who was completing basketball season and beginning track, followed them when he had time. He led from the first; a couple of other South students, Dorothy Gray and Siki McGee, lagged behind. By mid-March it was down to a two-man contest between him and John Prendergast of Central, and in the end Jerry won with over 15,000 votes.

The prize, a weeklong trip to Washington, D.C., was a real treat for a high-school student who was absorbed with history and public affairs. He did not take the option of going during the school year; there was simply too much to do as an athlete and a senior. In June, however, he joined twenty other Midwestern high school kids, contest winners like himself, at Chicago's Union Station for the overnight trip on the Pennsylvania Railroad, with first-class meals in the dining car, to the nation's capital. They had a thrilling time touring the White House, the monuments, the Supreme Court (still in the Capitol building), and the houses of Congress. As they stood in the

gallery of the vast, empty House chamber, where Ford was later to spend most of his working life, his thoughts were not on a political career. More likely, he was consumed by the residual excitement of graduating two weeks earlier and by the uncertainties of the deepening economic crisis. Later in life, he was to recall himself standing up there as a high-school graduate, watching the House in session. But he was mistaken about that. Congress did not meet that year until December, leaving President Hoover to handle the "Depression," as he was calling it.

Near the Capitol Mall, in the direction of the White House, Jerry and his group could see new government buildings going up for the Departments of Commerce and Justice, as Hoover did what he could to create jobs. On July 1, outside the House Office Building, they had their group picture taken, with Jerry, in rolled-up shirtsleeves, adapting to the broiling heat of an un-air-conditioned Washington summer. That picture would be the last in a long series that defined his senior year and tracked some of his responsibilities as a student leader. The series began in fall with the yearbook pictures. Jerry chaired the committee that was responsible for getting them back within a reasonable time, and they actually had them in graduates' hands before Christmas.

"Most popular" high school students at the U.S. Capitol, July 1931; Ford at center in white shirt

Then came the club and committee photos. In his block *S* sweater, he stood in the back row of the Varsity Club picture, in his usual spot between Art Brown and Swede Zylstra. Student Council and Sodalitas Latina, the Latin club, evidently had their photos taken the same day, because Jerry wore the same clothes in both: coat, vest, and a distinctive watch fob, a pretty swanky outfit altogether. He probably chose it in honor of his membership on the student council, which was a new experiment that year, supposedly getting students involved in school administration. In practice, it mostly meant monitoring the halls to catch wandering underclassmen without passes. Ford did his share of that work, and it earned him a line in the *Pioneer,* the yearbook: "Policeman — that's what Gerald Ford wants to be, when he grows up."

In fact, they were all growing up too fast in that Depression spring of 1931. Right after the Varsity Club dance, Art Brown dropped out of school to help support his family, and so did Siki McGee. Available jobs seemed fewer and fewer. Factories had cut back, and a man of ordinary skills had little chance of being hired. Some students were talking of a year in junior college until the economic situation got better, but as 1931 began, it seemed to be deteriorating further rather than improving. Even in Grand Rapids, even among young people, discussion of the situation was agonized and intense. "We had no idea what tomorrow might bring," one student recalled. Local people's theories about the cause of the downturn included millionaires' greed, "Russian Reds," and the system itself in some indefinable way.

The South High *Pioneer*'s vision of the future for 1931 graduates

And why had the government proved unable to do something about it? As one college student put it, "I'd say I think the time has come for a bigger change than just replacing the top fellers. Times are ripe for an upset." This bewilderment forms the background for another tale of the class of 1931, involving Ford's friends if not Ford himself.

At South that year, a lot of revolutionary talk came from Sid Nadolsky, who was portrayed in a cartoon in the yearbook making an oration on a soapbox. Sid, who played a mean saxophone both in the school band and in several private groups, was a popular, voluble senior from the Russian Jewish neighborhood on South Division Avenue. He was nicknamed "Red" — but not in a hostile way — because he was a freethinker in religion as well as politics. He liked to horrify pious female students with a book entitled *The Great Jehovah,* which exposed contradictions and absurdities in the Bible, a publication of the American Association for the Advancement of Atheism. His best friends were a couple of boys named Sompolinsky, who had attended South and then dropped out.

In the winter of their senior year, Florence Johnson, whose father's drugstore on Division was a community nerve center, heard that Sid, the Sompolinskys, and others had had a visit from sinister Detroit radicals, who gave them literature and instructions on converting the masses. As the weather warmed that spring, local radicals began holding outdoor meetings and orating in public parks. The Grand Rapids police routinely broke up those gatherings. Then, early on the morning of May Day, there appeared a message in bright red paint on the front steps of South High School: "Stay Out of School May 1!" According to people who claimed to know and spoke about it long afterward, it was probably the work of Henry Sompolinsky, though no one took credit at the time. There were similar signs in red paint at other school doors — including Union High — some using the word "strike."

From this point on, the story becomes fragmented. Everyone knew — or had heard — something, but no student knew the whole

Some individual graduates' futures, according to the 1931 *Pioneer;* "Red" Nadolsky at top left

story. Mr. Krause, arriving at the school early on the morning of the painted steps, spotted the slogans and decided that he knew who the perpetrators were. Rather than making it an official matter, he contacted Mr. Wickett, adviser to the Varsity Club, who contacted Bob Todish, president of the club. At midmorning, Sid Nadolsky was suddenly surrounded by a group of Varsity Club members carrying hockey sticks. They escorted him to the front entrance, gave him a paving brick, and forced him to get down and scrape the red paint from the steps while they stood over him. Two or three other students were treated similarly at the other locations. Rumors spread through the school that the "Reds" had been soused in the showers at the gym and that one or more had been taken by car and thrown into Plaster Creek. Mr. Krause told the newspapers that the administration had had nothing to do with the incident. This was a false statement, because nothing of importance went on at South High without Krause's involvement. As for student leader Jerry Ford, the student enforcers who intimidated the "Reds" were all his friends, but no one recalled his participating in any of the day's events.

By contrast, Jerry's last recollection of his senior year came from a couple of his jock friends, Bob Eckhardt and Marshall Reister. On Decoration Day (now Memorial Day), when there were no classes at South High, the three went to a public golf course where you could play all day for three dollars. Jerry told his friends that he was not much of a golfer, and he proved it on one particular hole: the club twisted in his hands, and he hit a 200-yard drive at a right angle to the fairway. Marsh and Bob howled with laughter.

What the May Day incident did for him and his fellow high-school seniors was underscore the turbulence of the world into which they were graduating on June 16, 1931. The commencement took place in the new South High School auditorium, completed only that year. Grand Rapids was a city on edge, and not because of Detroit agitators. Serious unemployment had existed from as long ago as 1927, when furniture sales had begun to turn down. Some factories had let workers go then; others had closed within a year or two of 1931. The Rescue Mission, the Salvation Army, and the Welfare Union were confronting a tide of unemployed men. In 1929 the City Commission appointed a brash new city manager, George Welsh, who promised to carry on the city's tradition of involvement in community problems. He set up a work-relief program that by mid-1931 was getting attention all over the country. Welsh had 2,000 men working for the city, clearing obstructions out of the river, widening North Division Avenue, and shoveling snow in winter. They were paid in "scrip," city-issued money that was redeemable only at a "city store" for food, fuel, and merchandise. Welsh managed to corral local markets and dairies into his system. One of his suppliers, a chain of meat markets called Ryskamp Brothers, was understood to be close to Frank McKay, the state treasurer who was the boss of the city's Republican Party. Did that connection mean that Welsh was some kind of puppet of McKay? The Ford men, Jerry Sr. and Jerry Jr., knew about McKay, as did nearly every businessman in the city. But they had never dealt with him directly; their interest in city affairs at that point was more idealistic than political. Jerry Sr. voted Republican, and Jerry Jr. followed his father's politics; but neither of them was a party politician. (They could not have anticipated then that, fifteen years later, Jerry Sr., involved in an effort to reform the local Republican Party, would buy a handgun to protect himself against McKay's henchmen.)

Whatever the truth, the threat of social breakdown hung over the city, visible in dozens of signs, some curious, some ominous. Lone bandits robbed filling stations and grocery stores in daylight. Every week another retail store or two closed. The number of applications for marriage licenses fell to a low level not seen for thirty years. Abandoned real estate developments were overgrown with weeds. Wealthy residents of the Hill District quietly barricaded their front doors. This possibility was what made the speeches of the "Reds" so threatening: their readiness to help pull down a collapsing society and open the door to famine and murder in the style of socialist Russia.

At the Ford dinner table, the conversation was less apocalyptic and more practical. Orders for paint and varnish had fallen drastically. The boss had sliced his own salary and the workers' wages, with a promise to them to make up the difference when prosperity returned. Jerry Ford Sr. was out in his car every day trying to sell his paint to hospitals, sanatoriums, and hotels, since the residential market had collapsed. Not only that, he had been forced to take over the failing coal business of his nephew Harold Swain. But no one in the family was giving up; they were all discussing strategies and supporting one another. Dorothy was doing her part with household expenses, but it looked inevitable that the Lake Drive house would have to go: the mortgage payments were simply too high. With the whole suburban real estate market in free fall, they figured, it should not be too hard to find a cheaper house in the same area. (And so it worked out: in 1932 the older Fords moved to a house on nearby Santa Cruz Drive, where they lived for the rest of their lives.)

Jerry Jr. planned, once he was back from his trip to Washington, D.C., to work at the Crosby Street plant all summer. Those wages would pay for his books at the University of Michigan that next year. He would room in the cheapest place he could find, and would not count on any spending money beyond the minimum. In Ann Arbor, Jerry planned to take courses in history, government, and economics, his favorite subjects. Some of his professors, no doubt, would offer their views on the industrial crisis, what was wrong with the American economic system, and what reforms needed to be made. Some might even argue, along with the Reds, that the best remedy was to rebuild the whole system from the ground up. But such projects held little interest for Jerry. After all, he had been raised to see the crisis not as a systemic failure but as a challenge to be faced with toughness, flexibility, and loyalty, the way his parents had always confronted challenges in their lives. He was confident that he could overcome the economic challenges of the times. And there was always football. He looked forward to his freshman year at Michigan.

Conclusion

Jerry Ford was far from grown when he left Grand Rapids in 1931 to attend the University of Michigan. The next few years would be full of experiences that would further shape his character and personality, culminating in the ordeal of World War II.

His four years at Ann Arbor, ending with his graduation from that institution in 1935, were less spectacular than was his high school career. Perhaps his most remarkable achievement was that he managed to stay in college continuously for those four years, without dropping out for a semester or a year or more, as so many students were forced to do during the Depression — in order to try to make money to continue their education. Ford, during those four years, put together the small amounts he earned in a variety of jobs, got help from friends, family, and the athletic department to make it through the University of Michigan. In a real sense, he paid for every step of his way through.

His athletic career at U of M was characterized by high achievement and bad breaks. He won the Meyer Morton Trophy — a silver football — as the outstanding freshman player in his first year, and he was named the most valuable player on the Wolverines' squad as a senior. Under Coach Kipke's guidance, he performed at a high level through all four years. But for his first two years on the varsity (his sophomore and junior years at Michigan) he was the backup center behind Chuck Bernard, an all-American, and got very little playing time. His consolation was that the Wolverines went undefeated for those two years, and won the national championship both years, 1932 and 1933. When he finally started, as a senior, the team was so weakened by injuries and graduations that the 1934 season was one of the most wretched in the history of Michigan football. They lost to archrival Michigan State by a score of 16-0, and then to the great University of Chicago team of that era, 27-0. The team's morale was plunging, and this was the backdrop for a dramatic episode in the annals of collegiate sports and race.

As Ford told the story in his autobiography, one of the best receivers on that U of M team was a black track star named Willis Ward. "He and I were close friends — we roomed together on trips out of town — and our friendship grew even closer during our senior year." Prior to the Georgia Tech game that fall, the coach of that all-white school threatened that his team would walk off the field and forfeit the game if Ward would be allowed to play. Michigan officials tried to work out a compromise in which Ward would sit on the bench for the game if a Georgia Tech star would do the same. Jerry Ford felt that the whole thing was morally wrong, and he consulted his father, who told him that he should do what the coaching staff decided was the correct thing to do.

"Still unsatisfied," Ford said, "I went to Willis himself. He urged me to play. 'Look,' he said, 'the team's having a bad year. . . . You've got to play Saturday. You owe it to the team.' I decided he was right. That Saturday afternoon we hit like never before and beat Georgia Tech 9-2." (This story is told in a recent video entitled *Black and Blue*.)

THE INTELLECTUAL PART of college life was not a big factor in Ford's Ann Arbor experience. He studied hard and maintained a B average, with some C's and the occasional A. The concepts and vocabulary of his courses may have made a useful impression as preparation for law school, but no evidence suggests that he learned anything that interested or affected him deeply. Probably the most meaningful part of his years at Michigan, in terms of maturity and growth, was his membership in the campus chapter of Delta Kappa Epsilon, which he joined in the spring of his freshman year. At Michigan as elsewhere, the Dekes had the reputation of a party house, hospitable to athletes and wild escapades. It was very different from his home life and values, but Jerry found he liked it. He lived in the house on Geddes Road all three of his remaining years, becoming the house manager in his senior year, with the income and responsibility that position entailed. The brothers were young Midwestern men from sophisticated urban backgrounds and income levels slightly above his own. From them he learned the standard rites of manhood — the smoking, drinking, and sex — that had not been part of his home experience. He also acquired a self-confidence and smoothness that were to stand him in good stead for years to come. The friendships he made in DKE were among the closest and most durable of his life.

The two years after he graduated from U of M were probably the closest Ford ever came to deciding on a career in sports — but not as a player. He received offers from three professional football teams, including the Detroit Lions and Green Bay Packers, based on his stellar performance in the 1935 Shrine Bowl. But he turned them all down in favor of an assistant coaching job at Yale, which Kipke helped him obtain. As an assistant coach, he was in a milieu he liked, plus he was making good money, doing a good job, and was appreciated by his peers. He had every reason to continue. His situation could be compared to that of Oklahoma's legendary Bud Wilkinson, who followed the same path at the same time, coming from a big state university to an assistant coach's job in the East. Both Ford and Wilkinson had prolonged disagreements with their fathers about a career choice: the older Ford and the older Wilkinson felt that football lacked the solidity to make for a real career. In Wilkinson's case, the son won out; in Ford's case, his father persuaded him to try a summer of law school at Michigan, and that experience turned the tide in favor of law for Jerry. Over the next three years, with the same kind of methodical discipline that he had shown before, Coach Ford added the burden of Yale Law School courses to his regular job and earned a solid B.

The real contribution of Yale to Ford's development, however, was not so much in legal preparation but in the broader area of national and global issues. Ford had gone to Yale, he later recalled, as a narrow Midwesterner, proud to be unconnected with the problems of Europe and civilization as a whole. Yale and life in the Northeast refocused his attention. He read more, and he conversed with different people. He felt that he now understood current events, and specifically the looming war in Europe, in a more accurate way. Like another Michigander, Thomas Dewey, he was a boy from the heartland who had come to the East for enlightenment; but unlike Dewey, he wanted to go back home and share his new knowledge with his own community. Football was still important to him and always would be, but it was no longer the center of his life. That position was held now by the struggle for freedom and democracy. He returned to Grand Rapids in 1940, and his interview for the FBI the next year suggests his commitment. In 1941 the Federal Bureau of Investigation was not just a job: its image was that of a group of select, highly trained crusaders against corruption and injustice. By applying to join it, Ford showed that he was ready to slay some dragons, as he did that year by joining the insurgent movement in Kent County against the political control of Frank McKay.

World War II wrenched Gerald Ford and his contemporaries out of their civilian lives at the end of 1941. Ford joined the Navy and served four years in exemplary fashion. The carrier he served on, the *Monterey,* was in the thick of the Pacific Theater from late 1943 to December 1944 and earned thirteen battle stars. Ford rose from recreation officer to navigation officer, commanded large bodies of men, and earned near-perfect evaluations. But the war did little to alter his sense of who he was and what he wanted to do with his life.

Concentrated experience and pressure did nothing more than toughen and strengthen values that were already formed. More convinced than ever of the need for reform, Ford came home in 1945 ready to serve his country in a public career.

January 3, 1949: Gerald R. Ford Jr., having been elected to the House of Representatives from the 5th District of Michigan, took the oath of office as a U.S. representative in the chamber he had first visited in June 1931. It was an end and a beginning: an end to Ford's quest to use the principles his parents, the Boy Scouts, and what his schooling had taught him in a constructive way, and the beginning of a long and useful Washington career that culminated in the presidency of the United States. His moral education in Grand Rapids had helped him rise to that point. In the future it would help him guide the country through two and a half years of a deeply troubled era.

Index

Illustrations are indexed with **boldface** *page numbers.*

African Americans, 28, 31, 35, 47, 93, 104, 128

Allaben, Joanna, 116

Athletes, high-school, 95-97

Automobiles, 1920s-1930s, 25

Badgley, Dr. Carl E., 101

Bernard, Chuck, 128

Berry, Virginia, 53, 83

Bill's Place, 15-16, **15**, 95

Bitely, MI, 77

Bloomer (Ford), Betty, 83

Bosscher, Harold ("Bosh"), 97

Boy Scouts of America
   in Grand Rapids, 25, 60
   Honor Guard at Fort Mackinac, 69-72, **70**, **73**
   merit badges, 64-66, **65**
   mission, 60
   Scout Law, **62-63**
   Scout Promise, 61
   Troop 15 (now 215), Grand Rapids, 61, 66

   uniform, 1927, **64**

Brown, Arthur, 95, 96, **98**, **105**, 106, 120

Burgess, Ted, **98**, **109**

Burghdorf, Orris, 90

Camp Shawondossee, 61-62, **66**, 67

Cherie Inn, 17, **17**

Christ Episcopal Church, Harvard, IL, 5

Churm, P. L. ("Pop"), 89, **100**

Conger, Gilbert, 76

Conger, Julia, 76

Conger, Ralph, 50, 76

Cook, Frank, **98**, 107, 110

Dauksza, Tony, 94

Delta Kappa Epsilon, 129

Demar, Alex, 80, 103

Depression, Great, 1929-1941, 38-39, 119, 120-21, **120**

Detroit, 57-58, 59, 121

Dood, Peter, 97, **100**

Dutch-American community in
Grand Rapids, 28, 31, 35-36, 58

East Grand Rapids, 29, 39, 102
Eckhardt, Robert, **100**, 104, 123
Elliott, Allan, 84-85, **85**, 95, **98**, 104,
105, 106, 107, 113
Engle, Art (neighbor), 46, 61
Engle, Ben (neighbor), 46, 61
English, Sylvia (neighbor), 46
Episcopal Church, 58

Football in 1920s, 87-88
anger management, importance
of, 90
center position, 88-89
high-school facilities and uniforms, 91-92
newspaper coverage of high-
school games, 93, 94, 98, 110
night games, 89
practice, importance of, 88
rules and equipment, 92, 106
Ford, Dick (brother), **8**, 14, 33, 39, **46**
Ford, Dorothy Gardner
birth of GRF, 1913, 5
Chicago, residence in, 8-9
child support, 7, 9, 19
clubs, 9, 14, 33, 60
cooking, 14, 15, 32-34
divorce from Leslie King, 7
domestic help, 34
drinking, opposed to, 59
entertaining, 34
Grand Rapids, moves to, 8-9
Great Depression, copes with, 125
health, 14, 33, 34
helps GRF with school, 42
marriage to Gerald R. Ford, Sr.,
10-11, 20, 60

marriage to Leslie King, 4-7
music, 34
as parent, 12, 13, 14, 18-19, 81, 83
personality, 14
photographs, **4**, **46**, **76**
in PTA, 42
religion, 9, 12, 58-59
scrapbook for GRF, 84, 95, **108**,
115
social activity, 14, 15
wedding, 1913, 3, **4**
Ford, Frances (grandmother), **11**
Ford, Gerald R., Sr. ("Jerry")
ambition, 23-24, 59
ambition for son, 54
car, 32, 113
character, 10, 24
choice of high school for son, 51
civic activity, 15, 26, 60
college costs, 111
described, 60
family background, 10
football camp, chaperones, 105
Grand Rapids Wood Finishing,
30, 32
Great Depression, copes with, 125
Horatio Alger, fondness for, 49
little time for kids' sports, 48
loses job, 30
Mason, 60, 111
meets Dorothy Gardner, 9-10
paint company, owns, 36-38, 99
as parent, 12, 18-19, 32, 34, 42-43,
101, 112, 129-30
photographs, **11**, **76**
in PTA, 42
religion, 12
Republican, politically inactive in
1930s, 124

Republican reformer in 1940s, 124

as salesman, 25, 32

Ford, Gerald R., Jr. ("Junior," "Junie," "Jerry") [GRF]

activities as teenager, 82, 85

admired by younger kids, 66, 81

adolescence, 36

adults, approved by, 80-82, 103, 117

Ann Arbor, visits, 101

appearance, 12, 61, 66, 87

athletics, serious interest in, 102, 113, 116, 129

awards, 94-95, 118

basketball, **100**, 111-12, 118

Bible verses memorized, 12, 19

Bill's Place, works at, 15-16, 95-96

birth, 5

boating, 68, 79

boyhood games, 32, 46-49

Boy Scouts, 25, 60-73, **56, 66, 70**, **73, 79**

bridge, 82, 85

Camp Shawondossee staff, 66-68, 90, 96

captain of football team, 97, 115

car, 79, 103, 112

character, 66, 80-82, 84, 117

civic issues, interest in, 53

coaching, as career, 129

coaching skills, 105, 106, 112, 129-30

company, preference for, 82, 84

dancing, 26, 81

dating, 83, 85

debating, 116

Eagle Scout, 66, 69-72, 89

elementary school, 41-44, 49, 117

encounter with Leslie King, 1930, 16-19

FBI, applies for position, 130

fighting, 49

fishing, 77

football (early), 48-49

football (high school), 18, 72, 82, 83, 85, 87-97; 1928 season, 90-94, **91**; 1929 season, 96; 1930 season, 105-8

football (college), 44-45

as football player, 89-90, 96-97, 106-7

football training camp, 104-5

Fort Mackinac Honor Guard, 69-73, **70, 71, 72, 73**, 96

girlfriends, 83, 85

girls, 48

golf, 13, 123

handwriting, 13, **44-45**

helps teammate with studies, 95

high school student, 53, 104, 115

history, interest in, 53, 104, 115

household chores, 32-33

injuries in childhood, 49

intelligence, 82

jobs as teenager, 15-16, 79-80, 103, 125

King, Leslie L. (biological father), 19

knee injury, 1929, 97

knee treatment and operation, 18, 97, 99, 101-2

law, interest in, 54-55, 115, 116-17, 130

leadership, 117, 123

learning style, 53

left-handedness, 13

manners, good, 81

May Day incident, 1931, 123

merit badges, 64-66

nicknames: "Jerry," 66-68

nicknames: "Junie," 68, 89

nicknames: "Junior," 8, 11-12, 15, 66, 68

opposes Frank McKay, 1941, 130

and Ottawa Beach, 75-77, 81

paint company, works at, 103

pastimes, 82

photographs, 2, **8**, 30, **40**, **46**, **56**, **70**, **71**, **72**, **73**, **74**, **76**, **79**, **85**, **86**, **91**, **98**, **100**, **105**, **109**, **114**, **119**

poetry, memorizes, 12, 53

popularity, 83, 84, 118

reading, 47, 49, 82

recruited by MSU, Harvard, Northwestern, 110

religion, 15, 85

Republican like father, 124

Republican reformer, 130

respect for father, 53, 68

responsibility, 80-81, 103

reticence as child, 13

roughness in football, reputation for, 90, 94

rules, respect for, 55

in Sea Scouts, 68

sensitivity, 82

South High School, sent to, 49-50, 53

speech problems, 13, 42, 54, 115-16

stamp collecting, 49

student government, 119, 120

study habits, 49

swimming, 26, **74**, 75-76, 113

temper, 12-13, 19, 90

track team (shot put), 95, 104, 113, 118

University of Michigan, chooses, 110-11, 113, 115

at University of Michigan, 11, 19, 44-45, 81, 82, 83, 125, 127-29

Varsity Club, 120, 123

Washington, trip to, 1931, 118-19, **119**

world affairs, views on, 130

in World War II, 130-31

writing style, 81

at Yale, 11, 130

Ford, Jim (brother), 14, 33, 35

Ford, Marjory (aunt), 11, 23, 26, 81

Ford, Tom (brother), **8**, 14, 49, 112

Ford family

car, 113

fishing camp near Bitely, MI, 77-79, 104-5

homes: 2163 Lake Drive, 39, 79, 102, **103**, 125; Madison Ave., 11, 24, 27-28; Rosewood Ave., 29-30; Santa Cruz Drive, 125; 649 Union Ave., 31-36, **31**, 43, 48

meals, 34

religion, 14-15, 34, 58-59

rode streetcars, 25, 83

Ford Paint and Varnish Company, 36, **37**, 38, **38**, 104, 110, 125

Fort Mackinac, **56**, 58

Gardner, Adele (grandmother), 3, 5, 8, **8**, 10

Gardner, Levi (grandfather), 3, 6, 7, 8

Garel, Burt (neighbor), 47-48, 54

Garfield Park, 106

Gettings, Clifford, 88, 90, 92-94, 95,

96, 97, **100**, 102, 105, 106, 107,
118
Goebel, Paul, 90
Grace Episcopal Church, 9, **10**, 11
Grand Rapids, MI
    All-City football team: 1928, 94;
      1930, **98**
    centennial celebration, 1926, 25,
      61
    churches, 57-58
    civic values, 57-59
    downtown, 23, 25-26
    economy, 21, 36
    Firehouse #7, 41, **43**
    football, popularity of, 87, 93, 107
    Grand River, 21, **22**
    Great Depression in, 120, 121,
      123-24
    Hill District, 22, 27, **28**, 39, 50, 59,
      124
    newspapers, 57, 93-94
    population in 1920s, 21
    public schools, 41, 50, 54; Central
      High School, 50-51; Creston
      High School, 92; Davis Techni-
      cal, 92; Jefferson School, 87;
      Madison School, 41, **42**, 43, 49;
      Ottawa Hills High School, 104,
      105-6
    railroads, 52
    rich, 59
    South Side, 28, 59
    transit system, 22, 25, 52
    West Side/East Side, 21-22, 29
Gray, Dorothy, 83, 116, 117, 118, 122
Green, Governor Fred H., 69, **70**

Heystek, Harry, Jr., 30
Heystek & Canfield, 10, 24-25, 30
Holland, MI, 75, 92, 93-94, 107

Hondorp, Mary, 83, 84, **84**, 96
Hopper, Georgia (neighbor), 46
housing in 1920s, 30, 31-33, 35-36
Hoyt, Charles, 101

Island Park, 91, 94

James, Gardner (cousin), 75, **76**
James, Jim (uncle), 75, **76**
James, Tannisse (aunt), 7, 75
Johnson, Florence, 121
Joslin, Leon, **100**, 104, **105**
Judd, Dorothy, 57

Kindle, Charles, 61, 65
King, Charles H. (grandfather), 4, 5,
    7, 9, **9**, 16
King, Leslie L. (biological father), 3-
    7, **6**, **9**, 16-18, 19
Kipke, Harry, 81, 101, 110-11, 127
Koepnick, Russ, 92
Koning, Bert, 94
Krause, Arthur W., **51**, 52, 68, 106,
    110, 123

LeValley, Roy R., 52
Linsley, Bessie, **52**

McGee, Silas ("Siki"), **98**, **100**, 104,
    106, 118, 120
McIntosh, Joe, **56**, 72
McKay, Frank, 124, 130
Mackinac Island, **68**, 69, 70-72
McNitt, James, 116
Malta Lodge, 60
Martin, Heinie, 94
Michigan Stadium, 101, **102**
Murphy, Margaret, 81
Muskegon, MI, 93

Nadolsky, Sid, 121-23, **122**
Nichols, Bill (neighbor), 81

Nichols, Don (neighbor), 81
Nichols, Leigh (neighbor), 77, **79**

Ottawa Beach, 75-77, **76**

Pantlind, Frederica, **44-45**
Pere Marquette River fishing area,
  77, **78**
Prendergast, John, 118
Preston, Edward, 106
Prohibition, 59

Ramona Park, 27, **28**, 79-80, **80**
Reed, Lucy, 53
Reeds Lake, 27, **28**, 39
Reister, Marshall, 123
Rose, Danny, 97, **100**, 99-101, 110,
  111-12
Russo, Joe, 88, 93, 97
Ryskamp Brothers markets, 124

St. Mark's Episcopal Church, 25, **26**,
  58-59
Schuiling, Bill, 85, 106, 117
Schumann, Carl, 36
Scottish Rite Masonry, 60
Simpson, Albert H., 32, **35**, 36, 38
Skougis, Bill, 16, 95
Slack, Bob, 67
Sompolinsky, Henry, 121
South High School
  Class of 1931, 83, **120**, 122, 123
  classes, 51
  curriculums, 54
  described, 50, 51-52
  football field, 1931, 105, 107
  football team: 1928, **91**, 92-94;
    1929, 97, 99, 104; 1930, 104-10;
    city football champion, 1928,
    94; city football champion,
    1930, 107, 110; second team,
    88-90; state football champion,
    1930, 107, 110
  football uniforms, 92
  location, 49
  May Day incident, 1931, 121-23
  neighborhood, 52
  pep rallies, 115-16
  student government, **114**, 117-18,
    120
  teachers, 52, 53
  Varsity Club, 120, 123
South-Union football game, 1931,
  107-10
Stiles, Fred, 110
Stiles, Jack, 82
"Stump Country," 77
Swain, Harold T., 28, **30**, 125

Todish, Bob, 123
Trimpe, Jim, 107

Union High School, 94, 110, 121
Union Station, **24**, 25
University of Michigan, 110-11

Van Tassel, Leo, 117-18
Vevia, Alice, 52

Ward, Willis, 128
Waterman, Reed, 103
Welsh, George, 124
Whinery, Kay, 81
Wickett, Howard W., 52, **100**, 123

YMCA, 26, **27**, **74**, 97, 113
Yost, Fielding, 101
Youth Commonwealth, 59

Zylstra, Richard ("Swede"), **105**, 106,
  120, 122